The Ultimate American Cookbook

A Treasury of Recipes

Table of Contents

INTRODUCTION

Welcome to **"The Ultimate American Cookbook: A Treasury of Recipes"!** This culinary journey will take you on a delectable expedition through the diverse and flavorful landscape of American cuisine. From the rugged barbecue pits of Texas to the seafood-rich shores of New England, this book is your passport to savoring the flavors and traditions of the Western United States.

Discover the iconic dishes that define each region, from the smoky goodness of Texan BBQ brisket to the delectable California roll, which symbolizes the fusion of cultures on the West Coast. Explore the rich cultural tapestry of the American kitchen, and learn how different ingredients and techniques have come together to create an unparalleled culinary mosaic.

In "The Ultimate American Cookbook," you'll find a collection of recipes that capture the essence of America's culinary heritage. Whether you're a seasoned chef looking for new inspiration or a home cook eager to explore the tastes of the nation, this book provides a comprehensive guide to the flavors that make the United States a true culinary melting pot.

So, tie on your apron, gather your ingredients, and let the flavors of the Western U.S. inspire your culinary adventures. From coast to coast, this cookbook will become your go-to resource for mastering American classics and discovering regional specialties. Get ready to embark on an unforgettable gastronomic journey, one recipe at a time.

CHAPTER I
Western U.S

1.1 California: Fish Tacos

Fish Tacos

Introduction to the Dish:

California Fish Tacos are a delicious and popular dish originating from the coastal state of California. These tacos are known for their fresh and vibrant flavors. Crispy beer-battered fish is wrapped in warm corn tortillas and topped with a zesty cabbage slaw, making it a perfect blend of textures and tastes. These tacos are perfect for a family dinner or a casual gathering with friends.

Ingredients:

- 1 lb (450g) white fish fillets (such as cod or tilapia)
- 1 cup all-purpose flour
- 1 cup beer (for the batter)
- 1/2 tsp salt
- 1/2 tsp black pepper
- 1/2 tsp paprika
- 1/2 tsp garlic powder
- 1 cup shredded cabbage
- 1/2 cup sour cream
- 1/2 cup mayonnaise
- 1 lime, juiced
- 8 small corn tortillas
- 1 cup diced tomatoes
- 1/2 cup diced red onion
- 1/4 cup chopped fresh cilantro
- Sliced jalapeños (optional)
- Lime wedges for serving

Step-by-Step Instructions:

Batter and Fry the Fish:

- In a bowl, combine the flour, salt, black pepper, paprika, and garlic powder.
- Gradually whisk in the beer until the batter is smooth and lump-free.
- Cut the fish fillets into small, manageable pieces.
- Dip each piece of fish into the batter, allowing any excess to drip off.
- Heat oil in a deep skillet or pan over medium-high heat (350°F/180°C).
- Carefully add the battered fish pieces to the hot oil and fry until golden brown and crispy, about 3-4 minutes per side.
- Place the fried fish on a paper towel-lined plate to remove excess oil.

Prepare the Slaw:

In a mixing bowl, combine the shredded cabbage, sour cream, mayonnaise, and lime juice. Mix well and season with salt and pepper to taste.

- Heat the corn tortillas in a dry skillet or microwave until warm.
- Place a generous spoonful of the slaw on each tortilla.
- Add a piece or two of the crispy fish on top of the slaw.
- Garnish with diced tomatoes, red onion, fresh cilantro, and sliced jalapeños if you like some heat.
- Serve the fish tacos with lime wedges on the side for an extra zesty kick.

<u>Tips:</u>

- Use fresh and firm fish for the best results.
- You can customize the slaw with ingredients like avocado, radishes, or red cabbage.
- If you want a spicier kick, consider adding a spicy mayo or a hot sauce drizzle.
- Serve the tacos with your favorite salsa for an extra burst of flavor.
- For a healthier twist, you can also grill the fish instead of frying it.

Enjoy your homemade California Fish Tacos, a taste of the West Coast in your own kitchen!

1.2 Texas: Chicken Fried Chicken

Chicken Fried Chicken

<u>**Introduction to the Dish:**</u>

Texas Chicken Fried Chicken is a classic Southern comfort food dish with a Texan twist. It features tender, juicy chicken breasts coated in a crispy, flavorful breading and fried to a golden perfection. Served with creamy gravy, mashed potatoes, and your favorite vegetables, this dish is the ultimate Southern indulgence, perfect for a hearty family dinner.

Ingredients:

- 4 boneless, skinless chicken breasts
- 2 cups all-purpose flour
- 2 tsp salt
- 1 tsp black pepper
- 1/2 tsp paprika
- 1/2 tsp garlic powder
- 2 cups buttermilk
- Vegetable oil for frying
- Gravy (for serving, optional)
- Mashed potatoes (for serving, optional)
- Green beans or other sides of your choice

Step-by-Step Instructions:

1. Prepare the Chicken:

- Place the chicken breasts between sheets of plastic wrap or in a plastic bag.
- Pound the chicken to an even thickness of about 1/2 inch using a meat mallet or rolling pin.
- Season the chicken with salt, black pepper, paprika, and garlic powder.

2. Coat the Chicken:

- In one shallow dish, place the flour.
- In another shallow dish, pour the buttermilk.
- Dip each chicken breast into the flour, coating it thoroughly.
- Dip the floured chicken into the buttermilk, allowing excess buttermilk to drip off.
- Coat the chicken again in the flour, pressing the breading onto the chicken.

3. Fry the Chicken:

- In a large skillet, heat about 1 inch of vegetable oil over medium-high heat (350°F/180°C).
- Carefully place the chicken in the hot oil.

- Fry each side for about 4-5 minutes or until golden brown and the internal temperature reaches 165°F (74°C).
- Remove the fried chicken from the oil and place it on a paper towel to drain excess oil.

4. Prepare the Gravy (Optional):

- In the same skillet, pour off most of the oil, leaving about 2 tablespoons.
- Add 2 tablespoons of flour to the skillet and stir to create a roux.
- Gradually whisk in 2 cups of milk.
- Cook the gravy, stirring, until it thickens. Season with salt and pepper.

5. Serve:
Serve the fried chicken hot with gravy, mashed potatoes, and your choice of side vegetables.

Tips:

- Use a meat thermometer to ensure the chicken is cooked to the correct temperature to avoid overcooking.
- You can add a dash of hot sauce or cayenne pepper to the flour for a spicier version.
- Keep the fried chicken warm in the oven at 200°F (93°C) while you prepare the gravy and sides.
- For extra flavor, marinate the chicken in buttermilk with some hot sauce for a few hours before breading and frying.
- Customize your sides to your liking, but the classic combination includes mashed potatoes and green beans.

Enjoy your Texas Chicken Fried Chicken, a Southern delight that's sure to satisfy your taste buds!

1.3 Arizona: Green Chili Enchiladas

Arizona: Green Chili Enchiladas

Introduction to the Dish:

Arizona Green Chili Enchiladas are a delicious and mildly spicy Southwestern dish that celebrates the flavors of the region. These enchiladas are made with shredded chicken, green chilies, and a creamy, tangy sauce. They're baked to perfection and then garnished with cilantro and red onion, creating a flavorful and comforting meal.

Ingredients:

- 2 cups cooked and shredded chicken (you can use rotisserie chicken)
- 1 cup diced green chilies (canned or fresh)
- 2 cups shredded Monterey Jack cheese
- 8-10 corn or flour tortillas
- 2 cups green enchilada sauce
- 1/2 cup sour cream
- 1/2 cup chopped fresh cilantro
- 1/2 cup diced red onion
- 1 teaspoon ground cumin
- Salt and pepper to taste
- Cooking oil for heating tortillas
- Sliced black olives (optional, for garnish)

Step-by-Step Instructions:

1. Prepare the Filling:

- In a mixing bowl, combine the shredded chicken, diced green chilies, ground cumin, and 1 cup of shredded Monterey Jack cheese.
- Season the mixture with salt and pepper to taste.

2. Assemble the Enchiladas:

- Preheat your oven to 350°F (175°C).
- In a separate bowl, mix the green enchilada sauce with sour cream.
- Warm the tortillas in a skillet with a little cooking oil, just until they are pliable, then drain them on paper towels.
- Lay out each tortilla and fill it with the chicken and green chili mixture.
- Roll up the tortilla and place it seam side down in a baking dish.
- Continue this process until all the tortillas are filled and rolled.
- Pour the green enchilada sauce and sour cream mixture evenly over the enchiladas.

- Sliced jalapeños (optional, for added heat)
- Sprinkle the remaining shredded Monterey Jack cheese on top.

3. Bake the Enchiladas:

- Cover the baking dish with aluminum foil.
- Bake the enchiladas in the preheated oven for 20-25 minutes, or until the cheese is melted and the enchiladas are heated through.

4. Serve and Garnish:

- Remove the enchiladas from the oven and let them cool for a few minutes.
- Garnish with chopped cilantro, diced red onion, sliced black olives, and sliced jalapeños, if desired.
- Serve hot and enjoy your Arizona Green Chili Enchiladas!

Tips:

- Adjust the level of spiciness by using milder or hotter green chilies or by adding more jalapeños.
- Feel free to customize your enchiladas with other ingredients like black beans, corn, or diced tomatoes.
- Warm your tortillas slightly before filling to make them more pliable and easier to roll.
- Use corn tortillas for an authentic touch, but flour tortillas work well too.
- If you prefer a vegetarian version, you can replace the chicken with sautéed vegetables or black beans.

1.4 Oregon: Salmon Chowder

Oregon Salmon Chowder

Introduction to the Dish:

Oregon Salmon Chowder is a hearty and flavorful soup that pays homage to the Pacific Northwest's love for seafood. This chowder features fresh salmon, potatoes, and a medley of vegetables, all simmered in a creamy, savory broth. It's a comforting and satisfying dish, perfect for a chilly day.

Ingredients:

- 1 lb (450g) fresh salmon fillet, skinless and boneless
- 2 tablespoons butter
- 1 medium onion, chopped
- 2 celery stalks, chopped
- 2 carrots, peeled and diced
- 2 cloves garlic, minced
- 4 cups chicken or vegetable broth
- 2 cups potatoes, peeled and diced
- 1 teaspoon dried thyme
- 1 bay leaf
- 1 cup whole milk
- 1 cup heavy cream
- Salt and black pepper to taste
- Fresh dill, chopped (for garnish)
- Oyster crackers or crusty bread (for serving)

Step-by-Step Instructions:

1. Prepare the Salmon:

- Cut the salmon into small, bite-sized pieces.
- Season the salmon with a pinch of salt and black pepper.

2. Sauté the Aromatics:

- In a large pot, melt the butter over medium heat.
- Add the chopped onion, celery, and carrots. Sauté until the vegetables are tender, about 5 minutes.
- Stir in the minced garlic and cook for another minute until fragrant.

3. Simmer the Chowder:

- Pour in the chicken or vegetable broth and add the diced potatoes, dried thyme, and bay leaf.
- Bring the mixture to a boil, then reduce the heat to low, cover, and simmer for about 15-20 minutes or until the potatoes are tender.

4. Add Salmon and Cream:

- Stir in the seasoned salmon pieces and cook for about 3-4 minutes or until the salmon turns opaque.
- Pour in the whole milk and heavy cream.

- Heat the chowder gently, without boiling, until it's hot and the salmon is fully cooked. Be careful not to overcook the salmon, as it can become tough.

5. Season and Serve:

- Remove the bay leaf and discard it.
- Season the chowder with salt and black pepper to taste.
- Ladle the chowder into bowls, garnish with chopped fresh dill, and serve with oyster crackers or crusty bread.

Tips:

- Use fresh, wild-caught salmon for the best flavor and texture.
- If you prefer a thicker chowder, you can mash some of the cooked potatoes in the broth to help thicken it.
- For extra depth of flavor, consider using homemade seafood or fish broth.
- Be cautious not to overcook the salmon, as it can become dry and less tender.
- Add a dash of hot sauce or a sprinkle of smoked paprika for a subtle kick of heat, if desired.
- Leftover chowder can be refrigerated and reheated; however, the texture of the salmon may change upon reheating.

1.5 Washington: Cedar-Planked Salmon

Cedar-Planked Salmon

Introduction to the Dish:

Washington Cedar-Planked Salmon is a Pacific Northwest specialty that captures the essence of the region's abundant salmon and lush cedar forests. This dish is a celebration of simplicity and natural flavors, with salmon fillets infused with the smoky aroma of cedar and complemented by aromatic herbs and zesty lemon. It's an elegant yet straightforward recipe that's perfect for a special dinner or a weekend barbecue.

Ingredients:

- 4 salmon fillets (6-8 oz each)
- Cedar plank, soaked in water for at least 1 hour
- 1/4 cup olive oil
- 2 cloves garlic, minced
- 1 lemon, thinly sliced
- 2 teaspoons fresh thyme leaves
- 1 teaspoon smoked paprika
- Salt and black pepper to taste
- Fresh dill, chopped (for garnish)
- Additional lemon wedges (for serving)

Step-by-Step Instructions:

1. Prepare the Cedar Plank:

- Soak the cedar plank in water for at least 1 hour, ensuring it's fully submerged. This prevents the plank from catching fire during cooking.

2. Preheat the Grill:

- Preheat your grill to medium-high heat (about 350-375°F or 175-190°C).

3. Season the Salmon:

- In a small bowl, mix together the olive oil, minced garlic, smoked paprika, fresh thyme, salt, and black pepper.
- Brush the salmon fillets on both sides with the olive oil mixture.

4. Grill the Cedar-Planked Salmon:

- Place the soaked cedar plank on the preheated grill for a couple of minutes to warm it up.
- Carefully flip the plank and place the seasoned salmon fillets on top of it.
- Arrange the lemon slices on the salmon fillets.
- Close the grill and cook for about 15-20 minutes, or until the salmon is cooked to your preferred level of doneness (usually until it flakes easily with a fork).

5. Serve:

- Carefully remove the cedar plank with the salmon from the grill.
- Garnish with freshly chopped dill.
- Serve the cedar-planked salmon with additional lemon wedges on the side.

Tips:

- Choose high-quality, fresh salmon for the best flavor. Wild-caught salmon is a great choice.
- You can marinate the salmon for up to 30 minutes before grilling for a more intense flavor.
- To add extra smokiness, you can use a combination of cedar and alder planks.
- Keep a spray bottle of water nearby while grilling to extinguish any flames that may arise from the cedar plank.
- Make sure the grill is at the right temperature; it should be hot enough to cook the salmon but not so hot that it ignites the cedar plank.
- The cedar plank can be reused a few times, but be sure to clean it after each use and store it in a dry place.

1.6 New Mexico: Red Chile Posole

Red Chile Posole

Introduction to the Dish:

New Mexico Red Chile Posole is a traditional Southwestern stew that has deep roots in New Mexican cuisine. This hearty and flavorful dish centers around hominy corn and pork, simmered to perfection in a rich, red chile broth. It's a comforting, soul-warming meal, often enjoyed on special occasions or as a family favorite. The combination of smoky, earthy flavors and vibrant chiles makes it a beloved dish in the region.

Ingredients:

- 1 pound (450g) dried hominy corn
- 2 pounds (900g) pork shoulder, cut into cubes
- 2 large onions, chopped
- 4 cloves garlic, minced
- 2 cans (14-ounce each) diced tomatoes
- 2 cans (4-ounce each) diced green chiles
- 4 dried red New Mexico chiles, stemmed and seeded
- 6 cups chicken broth
- 2 teaspoons ground cumin
- 1 teaspoon dried oregano
- Salt and black pepper to taste
- Garnishes (optional): chopped cilantro, sliced radishes, shredded cabbage, lime wedges.

Step-by-Step Instructions:

1. Prepare the Dried Hominy:

Place the dried hominy corn in a large bowl and cover it with water. Let it soak overnight to rehydrate. Drain and rinse.

2. Brown the Pork:

In a large, heavy-bottomed pot, heat a bit of cooking oil over medium-high heat.

Brown the cubed pork shoulder on all sides, working in batches if necessary. Remove and set aside.

3. Sauté the Aromatics:

In the same pot, add the chopped onions and cook until they are softened and translucent.

Stir in the minced garlic and cook for about a minute until fragrant.

4. Prepare the Red Chile Sauce:

In a separate skillet, toast the dried red New Mexico chiles over medium heat for a few seconds until fragrant.

Transfer the toasted chiles to a bowl of hot water and let them soak for about 15-20 minutes until they are softened.

Once softened, blend the chiles with a bit of the soaking liquid into a smooth paste.

5. Simmer the Posole:

- Return the browned pork to the pot with the sautéed aromatics.
- Add the diced tomatoes, diced green chiles, blended red chile paste, and the soaked hominy corn.
- Pour in the chicken broth.
- Season with ground cumin, dried oregano, salt, and black pepper.
- Bring the mixture to a boil, then reduce the heat, cover, and simmer for 2-3 hours, or until the hominy is tender and the pork is cooked through.

6. Serve:

Ladle the posole into bowls and garnish with chopped cilantro, sliced radishes, shredded cabbage, and lime wedges.

Tips:

- You can also use canned hominy to save time, but the flavor of dried hominy is worth the extra effort.
- Adjust the level of spiciness by adding more or fewer dried red chiles.
- Some variations of posole include adding other proteins like chicken or beef, so feel free to customize it to your preferences.
- Leftover posole often tastes even better the next day after the flavors have had time to meld.
- Traditional posole is typically served with a side of warm corn tortillas.

1.7 Colorado: Bison Chili

Bison Chili

Introduction to the Dish:

Colorado Bison Chili is a hearty and flavorful dish inspired by the Rocky Mountain state's love for bison. Bison meat is lean and rich in flavor, making it an excellent choice for a chili that's as delicious as it is nutritious. This chili features a combination of bison meat, beans, and a blend of spices, creating a warm and comforting meal perfect for cool Colorado evenings.

Ingredients:

- 1 lb (450g) ground bison meat
- 1 large onion, chopped
- 2 cloves garlic, minced
- 1 red bell pepper, diced
- 1 green bell pepper, diced
- 1 can (14 ounces) diced tomatoes
- 1 can (15 ounces) kidney beans, drained and rinsed
- 1 can (15 ounces) black beans, drained and rinsed
- 2 cups beef or bison broth
- 2 tablespoons chili powder
- 1 teaspoon ground cumin
- 1 teaspoon paprika
- 1/2 teaspoon cayenne pepper (adjust to your preferred level of spiciness)
- Salt and black pepper to taste

Step-by-Step Instructions:

1. Brown the Bison:

- In a large pot or Dutch oven, heat a bit of cooking oil over medium-high heat.
- Add the ground bison meat and cook, breaking it up with a spoon, until it's browned. Remove and set aside.

2. Sauté the Aromatics:

- In the same pot, add the chopped onion and cook until it becomes translucent.
- Add the minced garlic and cook for about a minute until fragrant.

3. Build the Chili:

- Return the browned bison meat to the pot with the sautéed aromatics.
- Stir in the diced red and green bell peppers and cook for a few minutes until they start to soften.

4. Add the Spices:

- Sprinkle the chili powder, ground cumin, paprika, and cayenne pepper over the meat and vegetables.

- Cooking oil for sautéing
- Grated cheddar cheese, sour cream, and chopped green onions for garnish (optional)

- Season with salt and black pepper.

5. Simmer the Chili:

- Pour in the diced tomatoes and beef or bison broth.
- Add the kidney beans and black beans.
- Stir well to combine all the ingredients.
- Bring the mixture to a boil, then reduce the heat, cover, and simmer for about 30 minutes to allow the flavors to meld.

6. Serve:

- Ladle the bison chili into bowls.
- Garnish with grated cheddar cheese, a dollop of sour cream, and chopped green onions, if desired.

Tips:

- Bison meat is lean, so be careful not to overcook it to prevent dryness. It's best when cooked to medium or medium-rare.
- Adjust the level of spiciness by adding more or less cayenne pepper, depending on your heat tolerance.
- Serve the chili with a side of warm cornbread or tortilla chips for a complete and satisfying meal.
- For extra richness, you can add a small piece of unsweetened chocolate to the chili during the simmering process.
- Bison meat is a healthy and sustainable choice, with a flavor that's somewhat similar to beef but a bit sweeter and milder. Enjoy the unique taste of the Rockies!

1.8 Nevada: Basque Sheepherder's Bread

Basque Sheepherder's Bread

Introduction to the Dish:

Nevada Basque Sheepherder's Bread is a rustic and hearty bread that traces its roots to the Basque shepherds who roamed the state's remote ranges. This bread is renowned for its simplicity and robust flavor, making it a staple in the traditional Basque cuisine of Nevada. The crusty exterior, soft interior, and fragrant topping of olive oil, garlic, and rosemary create a bread that's perfect for sharing with loved ones or complementing a variety of dishes.

Ingredients:

For the Bread:

- 4 cups all-purpose flour
- 1 tablespoon sugar
- 1 tablespoon salt
- 2 teaspoons active dry yeast
- 1 1/2 cups warm water

For the Topping:

- 1/4 cup olive oil
- 2 cloves garlic, minced
- 1 tablespoon fresh rosemary, chopped
- 1/2 teaspoon coarse sea salt

Step-by-Step Instructions:

1. Prepare the Dough:

- In a large mixing bowl, combine the flour, sugar, and salt.
- In a separate small bowl, dissolve the yeast in warm water. Let it sit for a few minutes until it becomes frothy.
- Pour the yeast mixture into the flour mixture.
- Stir to combine, and knead the dough on a floured surface for about 5-7 minutes until it's smooth and elastic. You may need to add more flour as you go to prevent sticking.

2. Let the Dough Rise:

- Place the dough in a greased bowl and cover it with a clean kitchen towel.
- Let it rise in a warm place for about 1-2 hours, or until it has doubled in size.

3. Prepare the Topping:

- In a small bowl, mix together the olive oil, minced garlic, chopped rosemary, and coarse sea salt. Set aside.

4. Shape and Bake the Bread:

- Preheat your oven to 375°F (190°C).
- Punch down the risen dough and shape it into a round or oval loaf.
- Place the shaped dough on a parchment-lined baking sheet.
- Brush the olive oil topping generously over the loaf.

5. Let the Bread Rise Again:

- Cover the bread with a clean kitchen towel and let it rise for another 20-30 minutes.

6. Bake the Bread:

- Bake the bread in the preheated oven for 30-35 minutes, or until it's golden brown and sounds hollow when tapped on the bottom.
- Remove the bread from the oven and let it cool on a wire rack.

7. Serve:

- Slice and serve your Basque Sheepherder's Bread. Enjoy its rustic, savory flavors!

<u>Tips:</u>

- Make sure your yeast is fresh and active for the best rise and flavor in your bread.
- You can customize the topping with other herbs or even a sprinkle of cheese for extra flavor.
- This bread pairs wonderfully with soups, stews, or as an accompaniment to a charcuterie and cheese platter.
- The key to a good crust is to preheat the oven and use steam. You can place a shallow pan of hot water in the oven while baking to create steam, giving the bread a crisp crust.

- Store any leftovers in an airtight container or plastic bag to keep the bread fresh. Reheat in the oven or toast for a delightful treat.

1.9 Utah: Funeral Potatoes

Funeral Potatoes

Introduction to the Dish:

Utah Funeral Potatoes, also known as Mormon Funeral Potatoes, are a beloved and comforting casserole dish that's often shared at gatherings and potlucks in Utah. The name may not sound appetizing, but this cheesy potato casserole is a true comfort food staple in the state. It consists of creamy, cheesy hash brown potatoes, a hint of onion, and a crispy cornflake topping. Funeral Potatoes are a warm and hearty dish that brings people together.

Ingredients:

For the Casserole:

- 2 pounds (about 4 cups) frozen hash brown potatoes, thawed
- 1/2 cup butter, melted
- 1 can (10.75 ounces) condensed cream of chicken soup
- 1 cup sour cream
- 1/2 cup diced onion
- 2 cups shredded cheddar cheese
- 2 cups cornflakes, crushed
- 1/4 cup butter, melted (for topping)
- Salt and pepper to taste

Step-by-Step Instructions:

1. Prepare the Casserole:

- Preheat your oven to 350°F (175°C).
- In a large mixing bowl, combine the thawed hash brown potatoes and melted 1/2 cup of butter.
- Stir in the condensed cream of chicken soup and sour cream.
- Add the diced onion and shredded cheddar cheese.
- Season the mixture with salt and pepper to taste.
- Mix everything thoroughly.

2. Prepare the Topping:

- In a separate bowl, crush the cornflakes and mix them with the remaining 1/4 cup of melted butter.

3. Assemble the Casserole:

- Grease a 9x13-inch baking dish.
- Spread the potato mixture evenly in the dish.
- Sprinkle the cornflake topping over the potatoes.

4. Bake the Casserole:

- Bake in the preheated oven for 45-55 minutes, or until the top is golden brown and the casserole is bubbly.

5. Serve:

- Let the Funeral Potatoes rest for a few minutes before serving.
- Enjoy this comforting casserole as a side dish or a main course.

Tips:

- You can customize the casserole by adding ingredients like diced ham, cooked bacon, or different types of cheese.
- If you prefer a crispy top, you can increase the amount of cornflakes and butter for the topping.
- Funeral Potatoes are often served as a side dish for gatherings, potlucks, and holidays. They pair well with ham, chicken, or turkey.
- If you're short on time, you can use pre-packaged shredded hash browns, which can save you some prep work.
- Leftover Funeral Potatoes can be refrigerated and reheated for another delicious meal.

1.10 Idaho: Potato Casserole

Potato Casserole

Introduction to the Dish:

Idaho Potato Casserole is a classic comfort food dish that celebrates the state's most famous crop: potatoes. This casserole is a hearty and creamy delight, featuring thawed hash brown potatoes, a luscious mixture of cream of mushroom soup and sour cream, diced onions, and plenty of shredded cheddar cheese. Topped with a crispy layer of buttery cornflakes, it's a beloved Idahoan dish often enjoyed at family gatherings and potlucks.

Ingredients:

For the Casserole:

- 4 cups frozen hash brown potatoes, thawed
- 1/2 cup butter, melted
- 1 can (10.75 ounces) condensed cream of mushroom soup
- 1 cup sour cream
- 1/2 cup diced onion
- 2 cups shredded cheddar cheese
- Salt and black pepper to taste

For the Topping:

- 2 cups cornflakes, crushed
- 1/4 cup butter, melted

Step-by-Step Instructions:

1. Prepare the Casserole:

- Preheat your oven to 350°F (175°C).
- In a large mixing bowl, combine the thawed hash brown potatoes and melted 1/2 cup of butter.
- Stir in the condensed cream of mushroom soup and sour cream.
- Add the diced onion and shredded cheddar cheese.
- Season the mixture with salt and black pepper to taste.
- Mix everything thoroughly.

2. Prepare the Topping:

- In a separate bowl, crush the cornflakes and mix them with the remaining 1/4 cup of melted butter.

3. Assemble the Casserole:

- Grease a 9x13-inch baking dish.
- Spread the potato mixture evenly in the dish.
- Sprinkle the cornflake topping over the potatoes.

4. Bake the Casserole:

- Bake in the preheated oven for 45-55 minutes, or until the top is golden brown and the casserole is bubbly.

5. Serve:

- Let the Potato Casserole rest for a few minutes before serving.
- Enjoy this comforting casserole as a side dish or a main course.

Tips:

- Customize the casserole by adding ingredients like diced ham, cooked bacon, or different types of cheese.
- For a bit of extra flavor, you can add finely chopped green onions or chives to the mixture.
- Potato Casserole is a versatile dish that pairs well with various proteins, making it a great choice for potlucks and holiday gatherings.
- If you're short on time, you can use pre-packaged shredded hash browns to save some prep work.
- Leftover Potato Casserole can be refrigerated and reheated, but the cornflake topping may lose some of its crispiness. Consider toasting it in the oven to regain that delightful crunch.

1.11 Wyoming: Bison Meatloaf

Bison Meatloaf

Introduction to the Dish:

Wyoming Bison Meatloaf is a hearty and flavorful twist on a classic American comfort food. Bison meat brings a lean, rich flavor to this dish, making it a favorite in the state of Wyoming, where bison roam the open plains. This meatloaf combines ground bison and beef with a blend of seasonings and a sweet and tangy glaze, creating a satisfying and wholesome meal that's perfect for family dinners or gatherings.

Ingredients:

For the Meatloaf:

- 1 pound (450g) ground bison meat
- 1/2 pound (225g) ground beef
- 1 small onion, finely chopped
- 1/2 green bell pepper, finely chopped
- 2 cloves garlic, minced
- 1 cup breadcrumbs
- 1/2 cup milk
- 1/4 cup ketchup
- 1 large egg
- 1 teaspoon salt
- 1/2 teaspoon black pepper
- 1/2 teaspoon dried thyme
- 1/2 teaspoon dried oregano
- 1/2 teaspoon dried basil

For the Glaze:

Step-by-Step Instructions:

1. Preheat the Oven:

- Preheat your oven to 350°F (175°C).

2. Prepare the Meatloaf:

- In a large mixing bowl, combine the ground bison, ground beef, finely chopped onion, finely chopped green bell pepper, minced garlic, breadcrumbs, and milk.
- Add the ketchup, egg, salt, black pepper, dried thyme, dried oregano, and dried basil.
- Mix all the ingredients until well combined. Be careful not to overmix, as it can make the meatloaf dense.

3. Form the Meatloaf:

- Shape the meat mixture into a loaf shape and place it in a greased baking dish.

4. Prepare the Glaze:

- In a small bowl, mix together the ketchup, brown sugar, and Worcestershire sauce.

5. Glaze and Bake:

- 1/4 cup ketchup
- 2 tablespoons brown sugar
- 1 tablespoon Worcestershire sauce

- Brush the glaze over the top of the meatloaf, reserving some for later.
- Bake the meatloaf in the preheated oven for 1 hour or until it reaches an internal temperature of 160°F (71°C).
- During the last 10-15 minutes of baking, brush on the remaining glaze.

6. Rest and Serve:

- Remove the meatloaf from the oven and let it rest for a few minutes before slicing.
- Serve the Wyoming Bison Meatloaf with your favorite sides.

Tips:

- Ground bison is lean, so the addition of ground beef helps keep the meatloaf moist and flavorful.
- Don't overmix the meatloaf mixture, as it can lead to a denser texture.
- You can customize the seasonings and glaze to your taste, adding ingredients like minced garlic or diced onions to the glaze for extra flavor.
- Serve the meatloaf with mashed potatoes and a vegetable side for a complete and satisfying meal.
- Leftover meatloaf makes great sandwiches the next day.

1.12 Montana: Beef Stew

Beef Stew

Introduction to the Dish:

Montana Beef Stew is a hearty and comforting dish that's perfect for the cold winters of Big Sky Country. This stew is packed with tender chunks of beef, a variety of vegetables, and a rich, savory broth. It's a beloved meal in Montana, where the beef is top-quality, and the stew is a symbol of warmth and hospitality. Whether enjoyed after a day of outdoor adventures or as a family dinner, this beef stew is a true Montana classic.

Ingredients:

- 1.5 pounds (680g) beef stew meat, cut into chunks
- 2 tablespoons all-purpose flour
- 2 tablespoons cooking oil
- 1 onion, chopped
- 2 cloves garlic, minced
- 4 carrots, peeled and sliced
- 4 potatoes, peeled and diced
- 2 celery stalks, chopped
- 4 cups beef broth
- 1 cup red wine (optional)
- 1 bay leaf
- 1 teaspoon dried thyme
- Salt and black pepper to taste
- Chopped fresh parsley for garnish

Step-by-Step Instructions:

1. Prepare the Beef:

- In a large bowl, toss the beef stew meat with the all-purpose flour, coating the meat evenly.

2. Brown the Beef:

- In a large, heavy-bottomed pot or Dutch oven, heat the cooking oil over medium-high heat.
- Add the coated beef chunks and sear them until they are browned on all sides. Remove the beef and set it aside.

3. Sauté the Aromatics:

- In the same pot, add the chopped onion and cook until it becomes translucent.
- Add the minced garlic and sauté for about a minute until fragrant.

4. Assemble the Stew:

- Return the browned beef to the pot with the sautéed aromatics.
- Add the sliced carrots, diced potatoes, and chopped celery.

- Pour in the beef broth and red wine (if using).
- Stir in the bay leaf and dried thyme.
- Season the stew with salt and black pepper to taste.

5. Simmer the Stew:

- Bring the mixture to a boil, then reduce the heat to low, cover the pot, and let it simmer for 1.5 to 2 hours, or until the beef is tender and the vegetables are cooked through.

6. Serve:

- Remove the bay leaf.
- Ladle the Montana Beef Stew into bowls, garnish with chopped fresh parsley, and enjoy the warm and satisfying flavors of Montana.

Tips:

- You can use a slow cooker for this stew if you prefer a hands-off approach. After browning the beef and sautéing the aromatics, transfer everything to the slow cooker and cook on low for 6-8 hours.
- The red wine adds depth of flavor to the stew, but you can omit it if you prefer a non-alcoholic version.
- Montana Beef Stew is even better the next day, as the flavors meld, so consider making it in advance.
- Serve the stew with crusty bread or rolls to soak up the delicious broth.
- Experiment with different vegetables or seasonings to customize the stew to your liking.

Salmon Bake

Introduction to the Dish:

Alaska Salmon Bake is a delightful and wholesome dish that celebrates the abundance of salmon in the Last Frontier. Alaska is known for its pristine waters and world-renowned salmon fisheries, making this dish a true emblem of the state. This recipe keeps it simple, allowing the natural flavors of salmon to shine, with a touch of lemon, garlic, and fresh herbs. The result is a succulent and aromatic salmon dish that captures the essence of Alaska.

Ingredients:

- 4 salmon fillets (6-8 ounces each)
- 1/4 cup melted butter
- 2 tablespoons lemon juice
- 2 cloves garlic, minced
- 1 tablespoon fresh dill, chopped
- 1 tablespoon fresh parsley, chopped
- Salt and black pepper to taste
- 4 lemon slices (for garnish)
- Aluminum foil

Step-by-Step Instructions:

1. Preheat the Oven:

- Preheat your oven to 375°F (190°C).

2. Prepare the Salmon Packets:

- Tear four pieces of aluminum foil, each large enough to wrap around one salmon fillet.
- Place each salmon fillet in the center of a piece of foil.

3. Prepare the Marinade:

- In a small bowl, combine the melted butter, lemon juice, minced garlic, chopped dill, and chopped parsley.
- Season the mixture with salt and black pepper to taste.

4. Marinate the Salmon:

- Spoon the marinade evenly over each salmon fillet.

5. Seal the Packets:

- Fold the foil over the salmon, creating a sealed packet. Make sure it's well-sealed to keep the flavors and moisture in.

6. Bake the Salmon:

- Place the salmon packets on a baking sheet and bake in the preheated oven for 20-25 minutes, or until the salmon flakes easily with a fork.

7. Serve:

- Carefully open the foil packets, allowing the steam to escape. Be cautious of the hot steam.
- Garnish each salmon fillet with a lemon slice.
- Serve the Alaska Salmon Bake with your favorite side dishes.

Tips:

- The foil packets help to lock in the moisture and flavors, creating a moist and tender salmon.
- You can customize the herbs and seasonings to your preference, using herbs like thyme or tarragon for variety.
- If you prefer, you can grill the salmon in the foil packets on a barbecue instead of baking.
- Serve the salmon with wild rice, steamed vegetables, or a fresh green salad for a complete and healthy meal.
- Be careful when opening the foil packets as they will release hot steam. Enjoy the fresh, natural flavors of Alaska in this simple and delicious dish.

Lau Lau

Introduction to the Dish:

Hawaii Lau Lau is a traditional Hawaiian dish that's a celebration of the islands' cultural diversity and natural abundance. Lau Lau is a flavorful and aromatic dish made by wrapping seasoned pork, butterfish (or a substitute), taro leaves, sweet potatoes, and lu'au leaves (taro leaves) in ti leaves or banana leaves. The parcels are then steamed until the ingredients are tender and infused with the natural flavors of the leaves. This dish embodies the spirit of Aloha and is a beloved part of Hawaiian cuisine.

Ingredients:

For the Lau Lau:

- 12 large ti leaves or banana leaves (if ti leaves are unavailable, banana leaves can be used)
- 1 pound (450g) boneless pork butt, cut into 1-inch cubes
- 1 pound (450g) butterfish (or substitute with cod or mackerel), cut into 1-inch cubes
- 2 cups taro leaves, chopped (if unavailable, you can substitute with spinach)
- 1 cup sweet potatoes, peeled and cubed
- 1 cup lu'au leaves (taro leaves), finely chopped

Step-by-Step Instructions:

1. Prepare the Leaves:

- If you are using ti leaves, trim the stems and any rough edges, and blanch them briefly in boiling water to soften. If using banana leaves, cut them into large rectangles and briefly pass them over an open flame to make them pliable.

2. Assemble the Lau Lau:

- Take one leaf and place a portion of lu'au leaves (taro leaves) in the center.
- Add a portion of sweet potatoes, followed by a few pieces of pork and butterfish.
- Season with a small amount of salt.
- Fold the leaves over the filling and wrap them into a tight bundle. Secure the bundle with cooking twine or banana leaf ties.

3. Steam the Lau Lau:

- Place the wrapped Lau Lau in a large steamer.

- Salt to taste

For the Ti Leaf Wraps:

- Cooking twine or banana leaf ties

- Steam the Lau Lau for about 3-4 hours, or until the meat is tender, and the leaves have become soft and translucent.

4. Serve:

- Carefully remove the Lau Lau from the steamer.
- Serve each Lau Lau bundle on a plate, allowing diners to unwrap the leaves and enjoy the delicious contents.

Tips:

- If ti leaves are not available, banana leaves make a suitable substitute. Just make sure to blanch or briefly heat them to make them more pliable and to impart flavor.
- The key to Lau Lau is the slow and gentle steam, which allows the ingredients to meld and the flavors to develop. Be patient during the cooking process.
- Lau Lau can be filled with variations of proteins and vegetables to suit your preferences. Some recipes use chicken, beef, or even vegetarian fillings.
- This dish is often made for special occasions and celebrations in Hawaii, so it's a wonderful way to share the spirit of the islands with family and friends.
- Remember to unwrap the Lau Lau carefully as the leaves and contents will be hot. Enjoy the unique and delightful flavors of Hawaii Lau Lau!

1.15 Oklahoma: Chicken and Dumplings

Chicken and Dumplings

Introduction to the Dish:

Oklahoma Chicken and Dumplings is a beloved comfort food dish that's hearty, soothing, and perfect for filling your belly and warming your soul. This dish is all about tender chunks of chicken, soft dumplings, and a creamy, flavorful broth. It's a classic in Oklahoma, where it's often enjoyed on chilly days or as a way to bring people together around the dinner table.

Ingredients:

For the Chicken:

- 1 whole chicken (about 4-5 pounds), cut into pieces
- 1 onion, peeled and quartered
- 2 carrots, peeled and chopped
- 2 celery stalks, chopped
- 2 cloves garlic, minced
- 2 bay leaves
- Salt and black pepper to taste

For the Dumplings:

- 2 cups all-purpose flour
- 1 tablespoon baking powder
- 1/2 teaspoon salt

Step-by-Step Instructions:

1. Cook the Chicken:

- Place the chicken pieces, onion, carrots, celery, minced garlic, bay leaves, salt, and black pepper in a large stockpot.
- Cover everything with water, bring to a boil, then reduce the heat to a simmer. Cook for about 45 minutes to an hour, or until the chicken is fully cooked and tender.

2. Make the Dumplings:

- While the chicken is cooking, prepare the dumplings. In a mixing bowl, whisk together the all-purpose flour, baking powder, and salt.
- Add the milk and mix until the dough comes together. Don't overmix; it's okay if it's slightly lumpy.

3. Shred the Chicken:

- Once the chicken is cooked, remove it from the broth. Allow it to cool, then shred the chicken into bite-sized pieces.

4. Prepare the Broth:

- 1 cup milk

For the Broth:

- 6 cups chicken broth (from cooking the chicken)
- 2 cups whole milk
- 1/2 cup butter
- 1/2 cup all-purpose flour
- Salt and black pepper to taste

- In a separate pot, melt the butter over medium heat.
- Stir in the all-purpose flour to create a roux. Cook and stir for a few minutes until it's a light golden color.
- Slowly whisk in the chicken broth and whole milk. Continue to whisk until the mixture thickens.
- Season the broth with salt and black pepper to taste.

5. Add the Dumplings:

- Drop spoonfuls of the dumpling dough into the simmering broth.
- Cover the pot and let the dumplings cook for about 15-20 minutes, or until they are cooked through and no longer doughy in the center.

6. Finish the Dish:

- Return the shredded chicken to the pot and let it heat through.
- Taste and adjust the seasoning if needed.

7. Serve:

- Ladle the Oklahoma Chicken and Dumplings into bowls and enjoy the heartwarming, comforting flavors.

Tips:

- Homemade dumplings are fantastic, but you can also use canned biscuit dough as a quick alternative.
- The roux for the broth should be smooth and lump-free. Be patient while whisking to achieve the right consistency.
- You can add other vegetables like peas, corn, or green beans for extra flavor and color.
- Leftover Chicken and Dumplings will thicken in the refrigerator, so you might need to add a bit more broth or milk when reheating.
- This dish is perfect for warming up on a chilly day or for bringing comfort to your dinner table any time of the year. Enjoy!

Runza Casserole

Introduction to the Dish:

Nebraska Runza Casserole is inspired by the classic Nebraska fast food favorite, the Runza. A Runza is a yeast dough pocket filled with seasoned ground beef, onions, and cabbage. This casserole captures those same delightful flavors but in a simplified and convenient form. It's a delicious and hearty comfort food dish that's perfect for family dinners or gatherings, offering a taste of the Midwest.

Ingredients:

For the Filling:

- 1 pound (450g) ground beef
- 1 medium onion, chopped
- 4 cups cabbage, shredded
- Salt and black pepper to taste

For the Dough:

- 1 package (2 1/4 teaspoons) active dry yeast
- 1 cup warm milk (110°F or 45°C)
- 1/4 cup granulated sugar
- 1/4 cup vegetable oil
- 1 teaspoon salt
- 3 1/4 cups all-purpose flour
- 1 large egg

Step-by-Step Instructions:

1. Prepare the Dough:

- In a small bowl, dissolve the active dry yeast in warm milk. Let it sit for about 5 minutes until it becomes frothy.
- In a large mixing bowl, combine the sugar, vegetable oil, salt, and 2 cups of all-purpose flour.
- Add the yeast mixture and the egg to the bowl. Mix well.
- Gradually add the remaining 1 1/4 cups of flour, kneading until the dough is smooth and elastic. This will take about 5-7 minutes.
- Place the dough in a greased bowl, cover it with a cloth, and let it rise in a warm place for about 1 hour, or until it has doubled in size.

2. Prepare the Filling:

- While the dough is rising, prepare the filling. In a large skillet, brown the ground beef and chopped onion over medium heat.
- Add the shredded cabbage to the skillet and cook until it's wilted and the mixture is well combined. Season with salt and black pepper to taste.

3. Assemble the Casserole:

- Preheat your oven to 350°F (175°C).
- Punch down the risen dough and divide it in half.
- Roll out one half of the dough into a rectangle, about 12x16 inches.
- Place the rolled-out dough in the bottom of a greased 9x13-inch baking dish.
- Spread the beef and cabbage filling evenly over the dough.
- Roll out the other half of the dough into a rectangle, about the same size as the first, and place it on top of the filling.

4. Bake the Casserole:

- Bake in the preheated oven for 25-30 minutes, or until the top is golden brown.

5. Serve:

- Let the Runza Casserole cool for a few minutes before slicing and serving.

Tips:

- The dough should be soft and elastic. If it's too sticky, you can add a little more flour while kneading.
- You can customize the filling by adding spices like garlic powder, Worcestershire sauce, or even cheese for extra flavor.
- Leftover Runza Casserole can be reheated in the oven or microwave. It also freezes well for future meals.
- Serve the casserole with your favorite condiments like ketchup, mustard, or hot sauce for an extra kick of flavor.
- Nebraska Runza Casserole is a wonderful twist on the classic Runza, making it a great dish to enjoy with friends and family.

1.17 South Dakota: Bison Stew

Bison Stew

Introduction to the Dish:

South Dakota Bison Stew is a hearty and wholesome dish that's a reflection of the state's rich heritage and appreciation for the great outdoors. Bison is a symbol of the American West and is a prized ingredient in this stew. This recipe combines tender chunks of bison meat with a variety of vegetables, creating a savory and comforting stew, often enjoyed after a day of adventure in South Dakota's natural beauty.

Ingredients:

For the Bison Stew:

- 1.5 pounds (680g) bison stew meat, cut into chunks
- 2 tablespoons cooking oil
- 1 onion, chopped
- 2 cloves garlic, minced
- 2 carrots, peeled and sliced
- 2 potatoes, peeled and diced
- 2 celery stalks, chopped
- 4 cups beef broth
- 1 cup red wine (optional)
- 2 bay leaves
- 1 teaspoon dried thyme
- Salt and black pepper to taste

For the Dumplings:

Step-by-Step Instructions:

1. Brown the Bison:

In a large, heavy-bottomed pot or Dutch oven, heat the cooking oil over medium-high heat.

Add the bison stew meat and sear it until it's browned on all sides. Remove the bison and set it aside.

2. Sauté the Aromatics:

In the same pot, add the chopped onion and cook until it becomes translucent.

Add the minced garlic and sauté for about a minute until fragrant.

3. Assemble the Stew:

Return the browned bison to the pot with the sautéed aromatics.

Add the sliced carrots, diced potatoes, and chopped celery.

Pour in the beef broth and red wine (if using).

- 1 cup all-purpose flour
- 1 1/2 teaspoons baking powder
- 1/2 teaspoon salt
- 1/2 cup milk

Stir in the bay leaves, dried thyme, salt, and black pepper.

4. Simmer the Stew:

Bring the mixture to a boil, then reduce the heat to low, cover the pot, and let it simmer for 1.5 to 2 hours, or until the bison is tender and the vegetables are cooked through.

5. Prepare the Dumplings:

In a mixing bowl, whisk together the all-purpose flour, baking powder, and salt.

Add the milk and mix until the dough comes together. Don't overmix; it's okay if it's slightly lumpy.

6. Add the Dumplings:

Drop spoonfuls of the dumpling dough into the simmering stew.

Cover the pot and let the dumplings cook for about 15-20 minutes, or until they are cooked through and no longer doughy in the center.

7. Serve:

Remove the bay leaves and discard them.

Ladle the South Dakota Bison Stew into bowls and enjoy the hearty and satisfying flavors.

<u>**Tips:**</u>

- The red wine adds depth of flavor to the stew, but you can omit it if you prefer a non-alcoholic version.

- Bison is lean, so the addition of beef broth and red wine helps keep the stew rich and flavorful.

- You can customize the seasonings and dumplings to your taste, adding ingredients like fresh herbs or spices for extra flavor.

- Serve the stew with a slice of fresh bread or cornbread for a complete and satisfying meal.

- South Dakota Bison Stew is the perfect way to celebrate the natural beauty and flavors of the region, whether you're in the heart of the state or dreaming of its breathtaking landscapes.

1.18 North Dakota: Lefse (Potato Flatbread)

Lefse (Potato Flatbread)

Introduction to the Dish:

North Dakota Lefse is a beloved and traditional Scandinavian flatbread that holds a special place in the heart of North Dakotans. Lefse, often associated with the state's Norwegian heritage, is a soft, thin, and slightly sweet flatbread made from potatoes. It's a versatile and delightful treat that can be enjoyed with butter and sugar, or used as a wrap for various fillings. Making lefse is not only a culinary tradition but also a way to connect with North Dakota's rich cultural history.

Ingredients:

- 4 cups russet potatoes, peeled and cubed
- 1/4 cup unsalted butter, softened
- 1 tablespoon granulated sugar
- 1/2 teaspoon salt
- 1/2 cup heavy cream
- 1 1/4 cups all-purpose flour, plus more for rolling
- Butter and sugar, for serving

Step-by-Step Instructions:

1. Prepare the Potatoes:

In a large pot, boil the peeled and cubed potatoes until they are fork-tender.

Drain the potatoes thoroughly and place them in a large mixing bowl.

2. Mash the Potatoes:

Use a potato masher or ricer to mash the cooked potatoes until they are smooth and lump-free.

3. Add the Ingredients:

While the mashed potatoes are still warm, add the softened butter, granulated sugar, and salt. Mix until well combined.

Gradually add the heavy cream and mix it into the potato mixture.

4. Incorporate the Flour:

Gradually add the all-purpose flour to the potato mixture, mixing until the dough comes together.

Knead the dough gently for a few minutes until it is smooth and elastic. If the dough is too sticky, you can add a bit more flour.

5. Divide the Dough:

Divide the dough into small portions, about the size of golf balls.

6. Roll Out the Lefse:

Preheat a lefse griddle or a large, flat skillet over medium heat.

On a floured surface, roll out each dough portion into a thin, round flatbread. They should be about 12 inches in diameter.

7. Cook the Lefse:

Place the rolled-out lefse on the preheated griddle or skillet.

Cook each side for about 1-2 minutes or until it starts to bubble and lightly brown. Flip it and cook the other side.

8. Serve:

Remove the lefse from the griddle and place it on a clean kitchen towel to cool slightly.

Serve the North Dakota Lefse warm, either spread with butter and sprinkled with sugar or filled with your favorite sweet or savory ingredients.

Tips:

- Lefse is traditionally served with butter and sugar, but you can also enjoy it with jam, cream cheese, or even savory fillings like meat and vegetables.

- The key to rolling out lefse is to use enough flour to prevent sticking but not so much that it dries out the dough.

- Some people use a lefse turning stick to flip the flatbread, but a spatula works just as well.

- Lefse can be stored in an airtight container for a few days or even frozen for longer storage.

- Making lefse is not just about the delicious flatbread; it's a wonderful way to connect with North Dakota's cultural heritage and traditions. Enjoy the taste of this regional delicacy!

Green Chile Stew

Introduction to the Dish:

New Mexico Green Chile Stew is a beloved and iconic dish that celebrates the state's unique culinary heritage. New Mexico is renowned for its green chiles, and this stew is a flavorful showcase of their smoky, spicy goodness. Combining tender pork, roasted green chiles, and other hearty ingredients, this stew is a comforting and satisfying representation of New Mexican cuisine.

Ingredients:

- 1 pound (450g) pork shoulder, cut into 1-inch cubes
- 1 onion, chopped
- 3 cloves garlic, minced
- 2 cups roasted and peeled green chiles (Hatch or Anaheim), chopped
- 2 cups tomatoes, diced
- 2 potatoes, peeled and diced
- 4 cups chicken broth
- 1 teaspoon ground cumin
- 1/2 teaspoon dried oregano
- Salt and black pepper to taste
- Vegetable oil, for cooking
- Chopped fresh cilantro, for garnish (optional)

Step-by-Step Instructions:

1. Brown the Pork:

In a large pot or Dutch oven, heat a small amount of vegetable oil over medium-high heat.

Add the pork cubes and brown them on all sides. Once browned, remove them from the pot and set them aside.

2. Sauté the Aromatics:

In the same pot, add chopped onions and sauté them until they become translucent.

Add minced garlic and cook for about a minute until fragrant.

3. Add the Green Chiles:

Return the browned pork to the pot.

Stir in the chopped roasted green chiles. Adjust the quantity based on your desired level of spiciness.

4. Incorporate the Tomatoes and Spices:

Add the diced tomatoes to the pot and mix well.

Season the stew with ground cumin, dried oregano, salt, and black pepper. Adjust the seasonings to taste.

5. Add the Potatoes and Broth:

Toss in the diced potatoes and pour in the chicken broth.

Stir the stew to combine all the ingredients.

6. Simmer the Stew:

Bring the stew to a boil, then reduce the heat to low, cover the pot, and let it simmer for about 1.5 to 2 hours. The pork should be tender, and the potatoes should be cooked through.

7. Serve:

Ladle the New Mexico Green Chile Stew into bowls.

Garnish with chopped fresh cilantro if desired.

Tips:

- You can use either fresh or canned green chiles for this stew, but roasting fresh chiles imparts a smoky flavor that's authentic to New Mexican cuisine.

- Adjust the heat level of the stew by selecting milder or spicier green chiles.

- If you can't find fresh green chiles, you can use frozen or canned varieties, which are available in many grocery stores.

- New Mexico Green Chile Stew is often served with warm tortillas or crusty bread for a hearty and satisfying meal.

- Feel free to customize the stew with additional vegetables or spices to suit your preferences. Enjoy the rich and robust flavors of New Mexico in this delightful dish!

1.20 Arizona: Navajo Fry Bread Taco

Navajo Fry Bread Taco

Introduction to the Dish:

Arizona Navajo Fry Bread Tacos are a delightful and culturally significant dish that combines a crispy, golden fry bread base with a flavorful and customizable taco filling. This dish has its roots in Native American cuisine, specifically the Navajo Nation, and has become a beloved staple in Arizona and throughout the Southwest. The fry bread serves as a perfect vessel for your favorite taco toppings, making it a unique and delicious way to enjoy a taco.

Ingredients:

For the Fry Bread:

- 2 cups all-purpose flour
- 2 teaspoons baking powder
- 1/2 teaspoon salt
- 3/4 cup warm water
- Vegetable oil for frying

For the Taco Filling:

- 1 pound (450g) ground beef or ground turkey
- 1 small onion, chopped
- 1 clove garlic, minced
- 1 packet taco seasoning mix
- 1 cup lettuce, shredded
- 1 cup tomatoes, diced
- 1 cup cheddar cheese, shredded

Step-by-Step Instructions:

1. Prepare the Fry Bread:

In a mixing bowl, combine the all-purpose flour, baking powder, and salt.

Gradually add the warm water and mix until the dough comes together. You can use your hands to knead the dough gently.

Divide the dough into golf ball-sized portions and roll them into balls.

On a floured surface, roll out each dough ball into a thin, flat disc, about 1/4 inch thick and 6-8 inches in diameter.

2. Fry the Bread:

In a deep skillet or frying pan, heat about 1 inch of vegetable oil to 350°F (175°C).

Carefully slide the rolled-out dough into the hot oil, one at a time. Fry until the fry bread is golden brown and puffed, about 1-2 minutes per side.

- Sour cream and salsa, for garnish

Remove the fry bread from the oil and drain it on paper towels. Repeat for the remaining dough portions.

3. Prepare the Taco Filling:

In a separate skillet, cook the ground beef or turkey over medium heat until browned. Drain any excess fat.

Add chopped onions and minced garlic to the meat and sauté until the onions are soft.

Stir in the taco seasoning mix and prepare according to the packet instructions.

4. Assemble the Navajo Fry Bread Tacos:

To serve, place a portion of the taco meat on each fry bread.

Top with shredded lettuce, diced tomatoes, and cheddar cheese.

Garnish with sour cream and salsa, or any other favorite taco toppings you prefer.

Tips:

Be cautious when frying the fry bread, as hot oil can be dangerous. Use a thermometer to maintain the oil temperature and avoid overcrowding the pan.

The fry bread can be shaped into rounds, ovals, or any shape you prefer. The goal is to have a thin, evenly fried bread.

Navajo Fry Bread Tacos are highly customizable. You can choose your favorite taco fillings, including beans, guacamole, jalapeños, or any other toppings you enjoy.

Remember that fry bread is best enjoyed fresh and warm, so assemble your tacos just before serving for the crispiest texture.

This dish not only offers a wonderful taste of Arizona's culinary culture but also pays homage to the Native American heritage of the region. Enjoy your Navajo Fry Bread Tacos!

CHAPTER II
Eastern U.S

2.1 New York: New York Cheesecake

New York Cheesecake

Introduction to the Dish:

New York Cheesecake is a classic and iconic dessert that represents the culinary heart of New York City. This creamy and decadent cheesecake is known for its dense, rich texture and smooth, tangy flavor. It's often enjoyed plain or with a simple fruit topping, making it a delightful treat that's perfect for special occasions or anytime you crave a slice of indulgence.

Ingredients:

For the Crust:

- 1 1/2 cups graham cracker crumbs
- 1/4 cup granulated sugar
- 1/2 cup unsalted butter, melted

For the Filling:

- 4 (8-ounce) packages cream cheese, softened
- 1 1/4 cups granulated sugar
- 1 teaspoon vanilla extract
- 4 large eggs
- 2/3 cup sour cream
- 2/3 cup heavy cream

For the Topping (optional):

Step-by-Step Instructions:

1. Prepare the Crust:

Preheat your oven to 325°F (160°C).

In a mixing bowl, combine the graham cracker crumbs, granulated sugar, and melted butter. Mix until the crumbs are evenly coated.

Press the mixture into the bottom of a 9-inch (23 cm) springform pan, creating an even and firm crust. You can use the bottom of a glass or a measuring cup to press it down.

2. Make the Filling:

In a large mixing bowl, beat the softened cream cheese until it's smooth and creamy.

Add the granulated sugar and vanilla extract, then beat until the mixture is well combined.

Add the eggs one at a time, mixing well after each addition.

- Fresh berries, fruit compote, or fruit preserves

Stir in the sour cream and heavy cream until the batter is smooth and velvety.

3. Bake the Cheesecake:

Pour the cheesecake filling over the prepared crust in the springform pan.

Tap the pan on the counter a few times to release any air bubbles.

Place the pan on the middle rack of the preheated oven and bake for about 45-50 minutes, or until the edges are set, and the center is slightly wobbly.

4. Cool and Chill:

Turn off the oven and crack the oven door, allowing the cheesecake to cool slowly for about an hour.

Remove the cheesecake from the oven and refrigerate it for at least 4 hours, but preferably overnight to set.

5. Serve:

Just before serving, release the cheesecake from the springform pan.

If desired, top the New York Cheesecake with fresh berries, fruit compote, or fruit preserves.

Tips:

To prevent cracks on the surface of your cheesecake, make sure all your ingredients are at room temperature before you begin.

You can add a water bath to the oven while baking to help prevent cracks. Place a pan of hot water on the oven rack beneath the cheesecake.

When serving, dip a sharp knife in hot water and wipe it clean between each cut. This will help you achieve clean slices.

New York Cheesecake is incredibly versatile, so you can customize the topping to your liking, from chocolate ganache to caramel sauce or a drizzle of honey.

Enjoy your New York Cheesecake as a tribute to the rich culinary tradition of the state and the sweet delights of the Big Apple!

2.2 Maine: Lobster Bisque

Lobster Bisque

Introduction to the Dish:

Maine Lobster Bisque is a luxurious and indulgent soup that captures the essence of the Maine coastline. Known for its pristine waters and succulent lobsters, Maine is a seafood lover's paradise. This bisque is a creamy and velvety delight, brimming with the sweet, briny flavor of lobster. It's the perfect way to savor the taste of Maine's culinary heritage.

Ingredients:

- 2 live lobsters (about 1 1/2 pounds each)
- 2 tablespoons unsalted butter
- 1 onion, chopped
- 1 carrot, chopped
- 1 celery stalk, chopped
- 2 cloves garlic, minced
- 1/4 cup brandy (optional)
- 2 tablespoons tomato paste
- 1/4 cup all-purpose flour
- 4 cups seafood or lobster stock
- 1 cup heavy cream
- 1/2 teaspoon paprika
- Salt and black pepper to taste
- Chopped fresh chives, for garnish

Step-by-Step Instructions:

If you like it even hotter, drizzle with Sriracha sauce for an extra burst of flavor. 1. Prepare the Lobsters:

Bring a large pot of water to a boil. Gently place the live lobsters into the boiling water. Cover and cook for about 8-10 minutes, or until the lobsters turn bright red.

Remove the lobsters from the boiling water and let them cool slightly.

Crack open the lobsters and remove the meat from the claws, tail, and legs. Reserve the meat and any lobster juices.

2. Create the Lobster Stock:

In a large stockpot, melt the butter over medium heat.

Add the chopped onion, carrot, celery, and minced garlic. Sauté the vegetables until they become soft and fragrant.

If using brandy, add it to the pot and cook for a couple of minutes to cook off the alcohol.

Stir in the tomato paste and cook for another 2-3 minutes, or until it darkens in color.

Sprinkle the flour over the mixture and stir well to create a roux. Cook for a few minutes until the roux is light brown.

Gradually pour in the seafood or lobster stock, stirring constantly to avoid lumps.

3. Blend and Simmer:

Use an immersion blender to blend the mixture until smooth. Alternatively, transfer the mixture to a blender and blend until smooth, then return it to the pot.

Add the lobster meat and any reserved juices to the pot.

Stir in the heavy cream and paprika. Season with salt and black pepper to taste.

Simmer the bisque over low heat for about 15-20 minutes, allowing the flavors to meld together. Be careful not to boil it.

4. Serve:

Ladle the Maine Lobster Bisque into bowls.

Garnish with chopped fresh chives for a touch of color and flavor.

Tips:

You can enhance the flavor of the bisque by using the lobster shells to make a lobster stock. Simply simmer the shells in water for an hour, strain, and use the resulting stock in place of seafood or lobster stock.

Maine Lobster Bisque is a rich and decadent dish, so it's perfect for special occasions or a romantic dinner.

Don't overcook the lobster meat when boiling the live lobsters. It can become tough if cooked too long.

To make the bisque even more indulgent, consider drizzling a touch of sherry over each serving just before serving.

Enjoy the taste of Maine's coastal beauty with this elegant and delicious Lobster Bisque. It's a celebration of the state's culinary tradition and natural bounty.

Boston Baked Beans

Introduction to the Dish:

Boston Baked Beans are a quintessential dish that harks back to the rich culinary history of Massachusetts, particularly Boston. This hearty and flavorful dish features navy or white beans, slow-cooked to perfection with a delectable combination of molasses, brown sugar, and salt pork or bacon. It's a dish that has been savored for generations and represents the traditional New England cuisine.

Ingredients:

- 1 pound (450g) navy or white beans
- 1/2 pound (225g) salt pork or bacon
- 1 onion, chopped
- 1/2 cup molasses
- 1/3 cup brown sugar
- 1 teaspoon salt
- 1/4 teaspoon black pepper
- 1/4 teaspoon dry mustard
- 1/4 teaspoon ground cloves
- 1/4 teaspoon ground allspice
- 1/4 teaspoon ground ginger
- 1/4 teaspoon paprika
- 1/4 teaspoon cayenne pepper (optional)
- 1 teaspoon baking soda

Step-by-Step Instructions:

1. Prepare the Beans:

Rinse the beans in cold water and remove any small stones or debris. Soak the beans in cold water for at least 8 hours or overnight.

Drain the soaked beans and place them in a large pot.

Cover the beans with fresh water and bring them to a boil. Let them boil for about 10 minutes, then remove from heat. Drain the beans.

2. Precook the Pork:

In a separate pot, bring water to a boil and add the salt pork or bacon. Let it simmer for about 10-15 minutes to remove excess salt and fat. Drain the pork.

3. Prepare the Baking Mixture:

Preheat your oven to 250°F (120°C).

- 1/4 cup warm water

In a separate bowl, mix together molasses, brown sugar, salt, black pepper, dry mustard, ground cloves, ground allspice, ground ginger, paprika, and cayenne pepper (if using).

Cut the precooked salt pork or bacon into small pieces.

4. Combine the Ingredients:

In a bean pot or ovenproof casserole, layer the beans and the salt pork or bacon pieces.

Pour the molasses and spice mixture over the beans and pork.

Dissolve the baking soda in the warm water and pour it over the beans.

5. Bake the Beans:

Cover the bean pot or casserole and place it in the preheated oven.

Bake the beans for 6-8 hours, checking occasionally to ensure there is enough liquid. If the beans seem dry, you can add a bit more warm water.

6. Serve:

The Boston Baked Beans are done when the beans are tender and the sauce is thick and caramelized.

Serve the beans hot as a side dish, especially with traditional New England accompaniments like brown bread, coleslaw, or hot dogs.

Tips:

Soaking the beans overnight helps them cook more evenly and reduces the cooking time.

You can adjust the sweetness and spiciness of the beans to your preference by altering the amount of molasses, brown sugar, and spices.

Boston Baked Beans are even better when reheated, so feel free to make them a day in advance.

Don't rush the baking process; slow and low heat will yield the best results, allowing the flavors to meld and the beans to become tender.

Enjoy the taste of historic Massachusetts with this classic dish, which has been cherished by generations of New Englanders.

Pennsylvania Dutch Scrapple

Introduction to the Dish:

Pennsylvania Dutch Scrapple is a regional dish that reflects the culinary traditions of the Pennsylvania Dutch community, a group of German-speaking immigrants. This dish is known for its frugality and resourcefulness, as it makes use of various parts of the pig, including the leftovers. Scrapple is a hearty breakfast food that's made by simmering pork, mixing it with cornmeal, and then frying it to a crisp, golden brown. It's a true taste of Pennsylvania's heritage.

Ingredients:

- 2 cups cornmeal
- 4 cups water
- 1/2 pound (225g) pork shoulder or pork scraps
- 1/2 cup pork liver (optional)
- 1/2 cup finely chopped onion
- 1/2 cup finely chopped celery
- 1/2 cup finely chopped green bell pepper
- 1 teaspoon salt
- 1/2 teaspoon black pepper
- 1/2 teaspoon ground sage
- 1/2 teaspoon dried thyme
- 1/4 teaspoon ground marjoram
- 1/4 teaspoon ground savory
- Vegetable oil, for frying

Step-by-Step Instructions:

1. Prepare the Pork:

In a large pot, combine the pork shoulder (or scraps) and, if using, pork liver.

Add enough water to cover the meat, and then bring it to a boil. Reduce the heat and simmer for about 1-1.5 hours until the meat is tender.

Remove the meat from the pot and let it cool slightly. Once cool, finely chop the meat.

2. Create the Broth:

Strain the pork broth to remove any solids. You'll use this broth to mix with the cornmeal.

3. Mix the Ingredients:

In a separate bowl, combine the cornmeal and 4 cups of the pork broth. Stir to make a smooth paste.

Add the chopped pork, chopped onion, chopped celery, and chopped green bell pepper to the cornmeal mixture.

Season the mixture with salt, black pepper, sage, thyme, marjoram, and savory.

4. Cook the Scrapple:

In a large, deep pan, heat vegetable oil over medium-high heat.

Pour the scrapple mixture into the hot oil, spreading it evenly.

Cook until the scrapple becomes firm and browned on the bottom, about 10-15 minutes.

5. Cut and Serve:

Carefully flip the scrapple over and cook the other side until it's browned and crisp, about another 10-15 minutes.

Remove the scrapple from the pan and drain it on paper towels.

Slice the scrapple into squares or slices and serve hot.

Tips:

Scrapple can be a very personal dish, and variations in seasoning and ingredients are common. You can adjust the spices and pork types to your liking.

Scrapple is often served as a breakfast dish alongside eggs, toast, and condiments like ketchup or maple syrup.

You can refrigerate leftover scrapple and reheat it by frying it in a little oil or butter until it's crispy.

Scrapple is a dish that reflects a strong tradition of using all parts of the animal, making it a frugal and sustainable choice.

Enjoy a taste of Pennsylvania's history and the Pennsylvania Dutch culture with this unique and flavorful dish!

2.5 New Jersey: Pork Roll, Egg, and Cheese Sandwich

Pork Roll, Egg, and Cheese Sandwich

Introduction to the Dish:

The New Jersey Pork Roll, Egg, and Cheese Sandwich, sometimes affectionately called the "Jersey Breakfast," is a beloved regional favorite. It's a hearty breakfast sandwich that embodies the flavors and spirit of New Jersey. At its core, this sandwich features slices of pork roll (also known as Taylor Ham), fried eggs, and cheese, all lovingly nestled between a fresh breakfast roll. It's a satisfying and delicious way to start the day, and a true taste of New Jersey's culinary culture.

Ingredients:

- Pork roll (Taylor Ham)
- Eggs
- Cheese slices (common choices include American, cheddar, or Swiss)
- Breakfast rolls or Kaiser rolls
- Butter or cooking oil
- Salt and pepper (for seasoning)

Step-by-Step Instructions:

1. Prepare the Pork Roll:

Slice the pork roll into thin rounds. Some prefer to leave a small slit in the edges to prevent it from curling up while cooking.

2. Cook the Pork Roll:

In a skillet or frying pan, heat a little butter or cooking oil over medium heat.

Add the pork roll slices to the pan and cook until they become lightly browned and slightly crispy on both sides, about 4-5 minutes per side.

Remove the cooked pork roll from the pan and set it aside.

3. Fry the Eggs:

In the same pan, crack the eggs and fry them over easy or to your desired level of doneness. Season the eggs with salt and pepper.

Place a slice of cheese on each egg and let it melt slightly.

4. Assemble the Sandwich:

Split the breakfast or Kaiser roll in half.

Place the cooked pork roll on the bottom half of the roll.

Carefully slide the fried egg with melted cheese on top of the pork roll.

Cover the sandwich with the other half of the roll.

5. Serve:

Serve the Pork Roll, Egg, and Cheese Sandwich hot, ideally with a side of ketchup, hot sauce, or other condiments of your choice.

<u>Tips:</u>

Taylor Ham is a specific brand of pork roll, but in many parts of New Jersey, the term "Taylor Ham" is used to refer to pork roll in general. The name can vary depending on the region within New Jersey.

You can customize your sandwich with additional toppings like ketchup, mustard, hot peppers, or even a hash brown patty for extra crunch.

Many New Jersey diners and delis offer their take on the classic Pork Roll, Egg, and Cheese Sandwich, so you can explore various versions of this local favorite.

Some people prefer their eggs sunny-side up or scrambled for this sandwich, so feel free to adapt it to your taste.

Enjoy the iconic flavors of New Jersey with this delicious and satisfying breakfast sandwich!

2.6 Vermont: Maple-Glazed Ham

Maple-Glazed Ham

Introduction to the Dish:

Vermont Maple-Glazed Ham is a delicious and heartwarming dish that embodies the spirit of Vermont's famous maple syrup. Vermont is renowned for its high-quality, pure maple syrup, and this recipe brings that rich, sweet flavor to the forefront. This ham is perfect for special occasions, especially during the holiday season. The combination of sweet maple syrup and savory ham creates a harmonious balance of flavors that's sure to impress your guests.

Ingredients:

- 1 fully cooked ham (bone-in or boneless), about 5-7 pounds
- 1 cup pure Vermont maple syrup
- 1/2 cup brown sugar
- 1/4 cup Dijon mustard
- 2 tablespoons apple cider vinegar
- 1 teaspoon ground cloves
- 1 teaspoon ground cinnamon
- 1/2 teaspoon ground nutmeg
- 1/2 teaspoon ground allspice
- 1/2 teaspoon black pepper

Step-by-Step Instructions:

1. Prepare the Ham:

Preheat your oven to 325°F (163°C).

If your ham is bone-in, make shallow cuts (score) across the top of the ham in a crisscross pattern.

Place the ham in a roasting pan, cut side down.

2. Make the Glaze:

In a saucepan, combine the pure Vermont maple syrup, brown sugar, Dijon mustard, apple cider vinegar, ground cloves, ground cinnamon, ground nutmeg, ground allspice, and black pepper.

Cook the mixture over medium heat, stirring constantly until the sugar has dissolved, and the glaze is well combined. This should take about 5-7 minutes.

3. Apply the Glaze:

Pour a generous portion of the maple glaze over the ham, ensuring it coats the top and sides of the ham.

4. Bake the Ham:

Cover the roasting pan with aluminum foil.

Place the ham in the preheated oven and bake for about 10-15 minutes per pound. For a 5-7 pound ham, this would be around 50-75 minutes. Baste the ham with the glaze every 20-30 minutes.

5. Final Glazing:

During the last 10-15 minutes of baking, remove the foil to allow the ham to brown.

Continue to baste the ham with the glaze every 5-10 minutes until the glaze caramelizes, and the ham has a beautiful, golden-brown color.

6. Rest and Serve:

Remove the ham from the oven and let it rest for about 15-20 minutes before carving. This allows the juices to redistribute.

Slice and serve the Vermont Maple-Glazed Ham with any remaining glaze drizzled over the top.

<u>Tips:</u>

When purchasing the ham, you can choose bone-in or boneless, depending on your preference. Bone-in hams often have more flavor, but boneless hams are easier to carve.

Make sure to buy pure Vermont maple syrup for the best flavor. The quality of the syrup greatly affects the outcome of the glaze.

Save any leftover glaze to serve with the sliced ham or to use as a condiment.

Feel free to adjust the spices and seasonings in the glaze to suit your taste. You can add a bit more Dijon mustard for a tangier flavor or extra cinnamon for a spicier profile.

Enjoy the sweet and savory goodness of Vermont Maple-Glazed Ham as a tribute to the state's famous maple syrup and its culinary heritage!

2.7 New Hampshire: Clam Bake

Clam Bake

Introduction to the Dish:

The New Hampshire Clam Bake is a classic coastal feast that celebrates the bounty of the sea. New Hampshire's picturesque coastline is known for its fresh seafood, and this traditional meal is a beloved summer tradition. Clams, lobsters, corn, potatoes, and onions are cooked together in a pile of seaweed, creating a unique and flavorful experience. It's a culinary celebration of the state's coastal heritage.

Ingredients:

- Fresh clams (littleneck or cherrystone)
- Lobsters
- Corn on the cob
- Red potatoes
- Onions
- Melted butter
- Old Bay seasoning (or a similar seafood seasoning)
- Fresh lemon wedges
- Seaweed or rockweed (for steaming)

Step-by-Step Instructions:

1. Preparing the Pit:

Choose a suitable location for your clam bake, either at the beach or in your backyard. You'll need a fire pit or an open area where you can build a cooking pit.

Create a pit by digging a hole about 2-3 feet deep and lining it with large, flat stones.

2. Preparing the Fire:

Build a fire in the pit using hardwood, such as oak or hickory. Let the fire burn until it turns to hot coals.

3. Layering the Ingredients:

Once you have a good bed of hot coals, spread a layer of seaweed or rockweed on top of the coals. This will serve as the cooking medium and add a distinct ocean flavor to the food.

Place a layer of onions on top of the seaweed.

Add a layer of potatoes on top of the onions.

Layer the fresh corn on top of the potatoes.

Add a layer of lobsters on top of the corn.

Finish with a layer of fresh clams on top.

4. Covering and Cooking:

Cover the entire pile with more seaweed or rockweed. This will trap the steam and infuse the flavors.

Place a wet burlap sack or a wet, heavy cloth on top of the seaweed. This will help keep the steam inside.

5. Cooking Time:

Let the clam bake cook for about 1 to 1.5 hours. The cooking time will vary depending on the size of the pit and the amount of food. You'll know it's ready when the lobsters turn bright red, and the clams have opened.

6. Serving:

Carefully uncover the pit, remove the layers of seaweed and food, and place them on a large table.

Serve the New Hampshire Clam Bake with melted butter, Old Bay seasoning, and fresh lemon wedges for drizzling.

<u>Tips:</u>

Use fresh, live seafood for the best results. Be sure the clams are tightly closed, and the lobsters are lively.

Seaweed or rockweed is crucial for the traditional flavor, but you can substitute it with damp burlap or cheesecloth if you can't find seaweed.

Invite friends and family to participate in the clam bake experience, as it's as much about the process as it is about the meal.

Customize the ingredients to your liking. Some variations include adding sausage or other seafood like mussels and shrimp.

New Hampshire Clam Bake is not only a meal but a social gathering. Embrace the spirit of community and the flavors of the sea with this coastal tradition.

2.8 Connecticut: Steamed Cheeseburgers

Steamed Cheeseburgers

Introduction to the Dish:

Connecticut Steamed Cheeseburgers, often simply referred to as "steamed hams" or "steamed cheeseburgers," are a regional delicacy unique to the state of Connecticut. These burgers are prepared using a distinct method where the burger patties and cheese are steamed together. The result is a deliciously juicy and cheesy burger that's a culinary tradition in the Nutmeg State. It's a must-try for burger enthusiasts seeking a different take on this classic American dish.

Ingredients:

For the Burger Patties:

- 1 pound (450g) ground beef
- Salt and pepper, to taste
- For the Steamed Cheese Sauce:

- 1/4 cup finely grated sharp cheddar cheese
- 1/4 cup finely grated American cheese
- 2 tablespoons milk
- 1/4 teaspoon dry mustard
- 1/4 teaspoon paprika
- 1/4 teaspoon cayenne pepper (optional)

For Assembling the Burger:

Step-by-Step Instructions:

1. Prepare the Burger Patties:

Season the ground beef with salt and pepper and form it into small, thin burger patties. They should be thinner than typical grilled burger patties.

2. Prepare the Steamed Cheese Sauce:

In a small saucepan, combine the finely grated sharp cheddar cheese, finely grated American cheese, milk, dry mustard, paprika, and cayenne pepper (if using).

Heat the saucepan over low heat, stirring continuously until the cheese melts and the mixture becomes a smooth sauce.

3. Steam the Burger Patties:

To steam the burger patties and cheese sauce, you'll need a special steaming cabinet or a DIY setup. If you have a bamboo or metal steamer, that can work as well.

- Hamburger buns
- Lettuce, tomato, onion, and pickles (optional)
- Ketchup, mustard, and mayonnaise (optional)

Place the thin burger patties into the steaming cabinet or setup, leaving some space between them.

Pour the steamed cheese sauce over the burger patties.

4. Steam the Burgers:

Steam the burger patties and cheese sauce for about 10-15 minutes or until the burgers are fully cooked and the cheese is melted and gooey.

5. Assemble the Burger:

Place the steamed cheeseburger on a hamburger bun.

Add your choice of toppings, which may include lettuce, tomato, onion, and pickles.

Add condiments such as ketchup, mustard, and mayonnaise if desired.

6. Serve:

Serve the Connecticut Steamed Cheeseburgers while they are still warm, allowing the gooey cheese to ooze from the burger.

Tips:

You can find special steaming cabinets designed for making steamed cheeseburgers in Connecticut. These cabinets allow for consistent steaming and even distribution of the cheese sauce.

Experiment with the cheese combination in the sauce to suit your taste. Some people prefer using more or less sharp cheddar or American cheese.

If you don't have a dedicated steaming cabinet, you can use a bamboo or metal steamer basket as a DIY option. Make sure to adjust the setup to accommodate the burger patties.

Connecticut Steamed Cheeseburgers are all about the gooey cheese experience, so don't skimp on the cheese sauce!

Enjoy the unique and mouthwatering flavors of Connecticut with these delicious steamed cheeseburgers, a local specialty worth trying.

2.9 Rhode Island: Johnny Cakes

Johnny Cakes

Introduction to the Dish:

Rhode Island Johnny Cakes, also known as "journey cakes" or "johnnycakes," are a classic Rhode Island dish that traces its origins back to the indigenous Narragansett tribe. These simple yet delicious cornmeal pancakes have been a staple in Rhode Island cuisine for centuries. Johnny Cakes are a versatile dish, suitable for breakfast, brunch, or a hearty side. They are a culinary symbol of the state's rich history and tradition.

Ingredients:

- 1 cup yellow cornmeal
- 1/2 teaspoon salt
- 1/2 teaspoon sugar (optional)
- 1 cup boiling water
- 1/4 cup milk
- Butter or oil (for frying)
- Maple syrup, honey, or jam (for serving)

Step-by-Step Instructions:

1. Prepare the Johnny Cake Batter:

In a mixing bowl, combine the yellow cornmeal, salt, and sugar (if using).

Add the boiling water to the dry ingredients and stir until well combined. The hot water will help the cornmeal absorb the moisture.

Gradually add the milk to the mixture, stirring until it forms a smooth batter. The batter should be thick but pourable. Add more milk if needed.

2. Heat the Cooking Surface:

Heat a griddle or non-stick skillet over medium-high heat. Add a small amount of butter or oil and spread it evenly to coat the surface.

3. Cook the Johnny Cakes:

Pour a small amount of the Johnny cake batter onto the hot griddle to form pancakes of your desired size. You can make them thin or thick, depending on your preference.

Cook the Johnny cakes until they develop a golden-brown crust, which usually takes about 2-4 minutes on each side. You'll see small bubbles forming on the surface, which is a sign to flip them.

Flip the Johnny cakes and cook the other side until it's also golden brown.

Remove the cooked Johnny cakes from the griddle and keep them warm.

4. Serve:

Serve the Rhode Island Johnny Cakes hot with your choice of toppings. Traditionally, they are served with butter and maple syrup. You can also use honey, jam, or other toppings to suit your taste.

Tips:

Some variations of Johnny Cakes include adding a small amount of finely ground flint corn to the cornmeal, which can enhance the flavor and texture.

Experiment with the thickness of the batter to achieve the desired texture. Thicker batter results in denser Johnny Cakes, while thinner batter yields lighter pancakes.

If you prefer a slightly sweeter Johnny Cake, you can add a bit more sugar to the batter.

Traditionally, Johnny Cakes are served with butter and syrup, but you can get creative with toppings like fresh berries, whipped cream, or even savory options like bacon or cheese.

Enjoy the historical and comforting flavors of Rhode Island with these delicious Johnny Cakes, a dish that connects you to the state's culinary heritage.

2.10 Delaware: Chicken Pot Pie

Chicken Pot Pie

Introduction to the Dish:

Delaware Chicken Pot Pie is a hearty and comforting dish that's unique to the state of Delaware. It differs from the traditional pot pie in that it features a rich, flaky pastry crust on both the top and bottom, creating a sumptuous, double-crust pie. This dish is a tribute to Delaware's agricultural heritage, showcasing locally sourced ingredients like chicken, potatoes, and vegetables. It's a satisfying meal that warms both the heart and stomach.

Ingredients:

For the Dough:

- 2 cups all-purpose flour
- 1/2 teaspoon salt
- 1/2 cup cold butter, cubed
- 1/2 cup cold water

For the Filling:

- 2 to 2.5 pounds chicken, cut into pieces (bone-in or boneless)
- 4 cups chicken broth
- 2 cups diced potatoes
- 2 cups diced carrots
- 1 cup diced onions
- 1 cup diced celery
- 1/4 cup fresh parsley, chopped

Step-by-Step Instructions:

1. Prepare the Dough:

In a mixing bowl, combine the all-purpose flour and salt.

Add the cold, cubed butter and use a pastry cutter or your fingers to work the butter into the flour until it resembles coarse crumbs.

Gradually add the cold water and mix until the dough comes together. Form it into a ball, wrap it in plastic wrap, and refrigerate for at least 30 minutes.

2. Cook the Chicken:

In a large pot, place the chicken pieces and cover them with chicken broth.

Bring the broth to a boil, then reduce the heat and simmer for about 30-40 minutes, or until the chicken is cooked through.

Remove the chicken from the pot and let it cool. Once cool, shred or chop the chicken into bite-sized pieces.

- 1/4 cup fresh thyme leaves (or 1 tablespoon dried thyme)
- 1 cup frozen peas
- 1 cup frozen corn
- 1/2 cup all-purpose flour
- 1/2 cup heavy cream (optional)
- Salt and pepper to taste

3. Prepare the Filling:

In the same pot, add the diced potatoes, carrots, onions, and celery to the chicken broth. Bring it to a boil and simmer for about 10-15 minutes until the vegetables are tender.

Stir in the chopped chicken, fresh parsley, thyme, frozen peas, and frozen corn. Season with salt and pepper to taste.

If you prefer a thicker filling, mix 1/2 cup of all-purpose flour with a small amount of water to create a slurry. Stir the slurry into the filling to thicken it. You can also add heavy cream for a richer filling if desired.

4. Roll Out the Dough:

Preheat your oven to 350°F (175°C).

Divide the chilled dough in half. Roll out one half on a floured surface to fit the bottom of a deep pie dish.

5. Assemble the Pot Pie:

Pour the chicken and vegetable filling into the pie dish.

Roll out the other half of the dough and place it on top of the filling to create the top crust.

6. Bake:

Cut a few small slits in the top crust to allow steam to escape.

Place the pot pie in the preheated oven and bake for about 45-60 minutes, or until the crust is golden brown and the filling is bubbling.

7. Serve:

Allow the Delaware Chicken Pot Pie to cool for a few minutes before serving. Slice and enjoy!

<u>**Tips:**</u>

Delaware Chicken Pot Pie is traditionally made with a double crust, but if you prefer, you can make it with just a top crust.

Feel free to customize the vegetables to your liking. You can use different root vegetables, peas, or other veggies that you enjoy.

For a shortcut, you can use store-bought pie dough or puff pastry for the crust.

The chicken filling should be well-seasoned, as the pastry crust tends to be on the plain side. Adjust the salt and pepper to your taste.

Delaware Chicken Pot Pie is a wonderful dish to share with family and friends, especially during cold weather. Enjoy this hearty and flavorful recipe that's a tribute to Delaware's culinary heritage.

2.11 Maryland: Crab Imperial

Crab Imperial

Introduction to the Dish:

Maryland Crab Imperial is a beloved Chesapeake Bay classic and a seafood lover's delight. This dish highlights the sweet, delicate flavor of lump crabmeat by blending it with a rich and creamy mixture of mayonnaise, cheddar, mozzarella, and a dash of spices. Baked to golden perfection, Maryland Crab Imperial is a delightful appetizer or main course that captures the essence of Maryland's coastal culinary traditions.

Ingredients:

- 1 pound (about 2 cups) lump crabmeat, picked over for shells
- 1/4 cup mayonnaise
- 1/4 cup finely chopped onion
- 1/4 cup finely chopped celery
- 1/4 cup shredded cheddar cheese
- 1/4 cup shredded mozzarella cheese
- 1/4 cup panko breadcrumbs
- 2 tablespoons fresh lemon juice
- 1 tablespoon chopped fresh parsley
- 1 teaspoon Old Bay seasoning (or more to taste)
- 1/2 teaspoon dry mustard
- 1/2 teaspoon Worcestershire sauce

Step-by-Step Instructions:

1. Prepare the Crab Mixture:

In a large mixing bowl, combine the lump crabmeat, mayonnaise, finely chopped onion, finely chopped celery, cheddar cheese, mozzarella cheese, panko breadcrumbs, fresh lemon juice, chopped fresh parsley, Old Bay seasoning, dry mustard, Worcestershire sauce, hot sauce (if using), and salt and pepper to taste.

Gently fold the ingredients together, being careful not to break up the lump crabmeat. The mixture should be well combined but retain some texture.

2. Assemble and Bake:

Preheat your oven to 375°F (190°C).

Transfer the crab mixture to a baking dish or individual ramekins. You can choose a shallow baking dish for a large serving or smaller ramekins for individual portions.

Drizzle the melted butter over the top of the crab mixture in the dish or ramekins.

- 1/4 teaspoon hot sauce (optional)
- Salt and pepper to taste
- 2 tablespoons melted butter
- Lemon wedges and fresh parsley for garnish

Place the baking dish or ramekins in the preheated oven and bake for about 20-25 minutes or until the top is golden brown and the mixture is heated through.

3. Serve:

Remove the Maryland Crab Imperial from the oven and let it cool for a few minutes.

Garnish with lemon wedges and fresh parsley.

Serve this delectable crab dish as an appetizer with crackers or as a main course with a side salad or your choice of side dishes.

Tips:

Use high-quality lump crabmeat for the best flavor and texture. Be sure to check for and remove any shell fragments.

Old Bay seasoning is a signature spice blend from Maryland, and it adds a distinctive flavor to this dish. Adjust the amount to suit your taste, but it's an essential ingredient.

Don't overmix the crab mixture. Gentle folding will help preserve the texture and appearance of the lump crabmeat.

Maryland Crab Imperial can also be served as a topping for fish fillets or seafood-stuffed mushrooms. It's a versatile and flavorful addition to various dishes.

The hot sauce is optional and can be adjusted to your desired level of spiciness. If you prefer a milder taste, you can omit it altogether.

Enjoy the rich and delicious taste of Maryland Crab Imperial, a culinary treasure from the Chesapeake Bay that's perfect for special occasions or anytime you're craving seafood excellence.

2.12 Virginia: Virginia Ham Biscuits

Virginia Ham Biscuits

Introduction to the Dish:

Virginia Ham Biscuits are a classic Southern delicacy that celebrates the rich tradition of Virginia's country ham. These mini sandwiches are made with tender, flaky biscuits and thin slices of salty, savory Virginia ham. Whether enjoyed at a brunch, a picnic, or a Southern holiday gathering, these biscuits embody the essence of Southern comfort food.

Ingredients:

For the Biscuits:

- 2 cups all-purpose flour
- 1 tablespoon baking powder
- 1/2 teaspoon salt
- 1/2 cup (1 stick) cold butter, cubed
- 2/3 cup milk

For the Ham and Assembly:

- Slices of Virginia ham
- Mustard, mayonnaise, or honey for spreading (optional)

Step-by-Step Instructions:

1. Prepare the Biscuit Dough:

Preheat your oven to 450°F (230°C).

In a mixing bowl, combine the all-purpose flour, baking powder, and salt.

Add the cold, cubed butter to the dry ingredients. Use a pastry cutter or your fingers to work the butter into the flour mixture until it resembles coarse crumbs.

Gradually add the milk and stir until the dough comes together. Be careful not to overmix; the dough should be slightly lumpy.

2. Cut Out the Biscuits:

Turn the dough out onto a floured surface and gently knead it a few times to bring it together. Roll the dough to a thickness of about 1/2 inch.

Use a round biscuit cutter (about 2 inches in diameter) to cut out biscuit rounds. Gather the scraps, re-roll, and continue cutting biscuits until all the dough is used.

3. Bake the Biscuits:

Place the biscuit rounds on a baking sheet, leaving some space between each one.

Bake in the preheated oven for about 10-12 minutes or until the biscuits are golden brown and have puffed up.

4. Assemble the Biscuits:

Once the biscuits have cooled slightly, slice them in half horizontally.

Spread a small amount of mustard, mayonnaise, or honey (or a combination) on the inside of each biscuit half.

Layer thin slices of Virginia ham on the bottom half of each biscuit.

Place the top half of the biscuit on the ham to create a sandwich.

5. Serve:

Serve the Virginia Ham Biscuits warm or at room temperature. They are perfect for breakfast, brunch, or as a delightful appetizer.

Tips:

Virginia ham is known for its unique flavor and saltiness. Thinly sliced country ham is the traditional choice for these biscuits, but you can also use other types of ham if you prefer a milder taste.

You can customize the biscuits with condiments like mustard, mayonnaise, or honey, depending on your personal preference.

For a little extra kick, consider adding a thin slice of cheese or a pickle to your ham biscuits.

Virginia Ham Biscuits are a delightful addition to Southern gatherings, picnics, and special occasions. They're a true taste of Southern hospitality and tradition.

Be sure to store any leftover biscuits in an airtight container to keep them fresh. They can be reheated in the oven or microwave as needed.

2.13 West Virginia: Pepperoni Roll

Pepperoni Roll

Introduction to the Dish:

West Virginia Pepperoni Rolls are a regional specialty that combines the convenience of a hand-held snack with the irresistible flavors of pepperoni and cheese. These rolls have a deep-rooted history in West Virginia, where they were originally created for coal miners' lunches. The simple but delicious combination of fluffy bread, zesty pepperoni, and gooey cheese make these rolls a cherished treat in the Mountain State.

Ingredients:

For the Dough:

- 3 cups all-purpose flour
- 2 1/4 teaspoons (1 packet) active dry yeast
- 1 cup warm water
- 1 tablespoon sugar
- 1 teaspoon salt

For the Filling:

- 1/2 pound sliced pepperoni
- 2 cups shredded mozzarella cheese
- 1/2 cup grated Parmesan cheese
- 1/4 cup melted butter
- 1/2 teaspoon garlic powder
- 1/2 teaspoon dried oregano

Step-by-Step Instructions:

1. Prepare the Dough:

In a small bowl, combine the warm water, sugar, and active dry yeast. Let it sit for about 5-10 minutes, or until it becomes frothy.

In a large mixing bowl, combine the all-purpose flour and salt.

Pour the yeast mixture into the flour and mix until it forms a dough. Knead the dough for about 5-7 minutes until it's smooth and elastic. If the dough is too sticky, you can add a bit more flour.

Place the dough in a greased bowl, cover it with a kitchen towel, and let it rise in a warm, draft-free place for about 1 hour, or until it has doubled in size.

2. Assemble the Pepperoni Rolls:

Preheat your oven to 375°F (190°C).

Punch down the risen dough and divide it into smaller portions, about the size of a golf ball. You should have enough portions for the desired number of rolls.

- 1/2 teaspoon red pepper flakes (optional)

Roll each portion of dough into a small circle or oval.

Place a few slices of pepperoni and a generous pinch of shredded mozzarella cheese onto each piece of dough.

Fold the dough over the filling and seal the edges, creating a roll.

Place the rolls seam-side down on a baking sheet.

3. Make the Topping:

In a small bowl, mix the melted butter, grated Parmesan cheese, garlic powder, dried oregano, and red pepper flakes (if using).

4. Bake:

Brush the buttery topping over the tops of the pepperoni rolls.

Bake in the preheated oven for about 20-25 minutes, or until the rolls are golden brown and the cheese is bubbly.

5. Serve:

Let the Pepperoni Rolls cool for a few minutes before serving.

<u>Tips:</u>

You can customize the filling by adding other ingredients like sautéed onions, bell peppers, or different types of cheese to your liking.

West Virginia Pepperoni Rolls are often served at room temperature and are a popular snack for picnics, road trips, and school lunches.

If you want to make these rolls in advance, you can freeze them after baking. Simply reheat in the oven when you're ready to enjoy.

These rolls are wonderfully portable and are a favorite treat for those on the go. Consider packing them for your next outdoor adventure or as a unique addition to a party or gathering.

West Virginia Pepperoni Rolls are a culinary icon of the state, so embrace their heritage and share them with family and friends.

Cincinnati Chili

Introduction to the Dish:

Cincinnati Chili is a unique and beloved dish with a distinctive flavor that sets it apart from traditional chili. Hailing from Cincinnati, Ohio, this chili is often served as a topping for spaghetti and is commonly known as a "three-way" or "four-way" depending on the toppings. The secret to its complex flavor lies in a blend of spices, including cinnamon and cloves, which give it a sweet and slightly spicy profile. It's a regional favorite and an experience you won't want to miss.

Ingredients:

For the Chili:

- 2 pounds ground beef (or ground turkey)
- 2 large onions, finely chopped
- 4 cloves garlic, minced
- 2 cans (15 ounces each) tomato sauce
- 2 cups beef broth
- 2 tablespoons white vinegar
- 2 tablespoons Worcestershire sauce
- 2 tablespoons chili powder
- 1 1/2 teaspoons ground cinnamon
- 1 1/2 teaspoons ground allspice
- 1 1/2 teaspoons ground cloves
- 1 1/2 teaspoons cayenne pepper (adjust to taste)

Step-by-Step Instructions:

1. Cook the Meat:

In a large pot or Dutch oven, cook the ground beef (or ground turkey) over medium heat, breaking it up into small pieces as it browns.

Add the finely chopped onions and minced garlic to the meat. Continue cooking until the onions are soft and translucent.

2. Prepare the Chili Base:

Stir in the tomato sauce, beef broth, white vinegar, Worcestershire sauce, and all the spices: chili powder, ground cinnamon, ground allspice, ground cloves, and cayenne pepper. These spices are what give Cincinnati Chili its distinctive flavor.

Season with salt and black pepper to taste. Mix everything well.

Bring the mixture to a boil, then reduce the heat to low and let it simmer, uncovered, for about 1 to 1.5 hours. Stir occasionally.

3. Serve Cincinnati Chili:

- Salt and black pepper to taste

For Serving:

- Cooked spaghetti
- Kidney beans, cooked and drained
- Chopped onions
- Shredded cheddar cheese

When the chili is ready, you can serve it in several classic ways:

Two-Way: Serve over cooked spaghetti.
Three-Way: Add shredded cheddar cheese on top of the spaghetti and chili.
Four-Way: Add kidney beans on top of the cheese.
Five-Way: Add chopped onions on top of the beans.

Tips:

The spice blend is what sets Cincinnati Chili apart, so don't be afraid to experiment with the level of spiciness. Adjust the cayenne pepper to your preferred heat level.

Cincinnati Chili is known for its slightly sweet and savory flavor due to the spices like cinnamon and cloves. Don't skip these unique ingredients.

You can customize your chili by adding other toppings like sour cream or hot sauce to suit your taste.

Leftover Cincinnati Chili can be refrigerated and reheated for future meals. It's a versatile dish that can be enjoyed in various ways.

Be sure to serve this unique chili dish over cooked spaghetti and experiment with your favorite toppings to find your perfect "way" to enjoy it.

2.15 Kentucky: Hot Brown

Hot Brown

<u>**Introduction to the Dish:**</u>

The Kentucky Hot Brown is a legendary open-faced sandwich with a rich history dating back to the 1920s. This dish was first created at the Brown Hotel in Louisville, Kentucky. It's a delightful combination of flavors and textures, featuring sliced turkey, crispy bacon, and ripe tomatoes smothered in a creamy Mornay sauce. The dish is baked to perfection and then garnished with Pecorino Romano cheese, paprika, and fresh parsley. The Kentucky Hot Brown is a culinary icon of the Bluegrass State and is perfect for a hearty and indulgent meal.

Ingredients:

For the Sauce:

- 2 tablespoons butter
- 2 tablespoons all-purpose flour
- 1 1/2 cups milk
- 1/2 cup grated Pecorino Romano cheese
- Salt and black pepper to taste

For the Hot Brown:

- 4 slices of thick-cut white bread (toast points)
- 1 pound roasted turkey breast, sliced
- 8 slices of cooked bacon
- 2 ripe tomatoes, sliced
- Pecorino Romano cheese for garnish
- Paprika for garnish
- Fresh parsley for garnish

Step-by-Step Instructions:

1. Prepare the Mornay Sauce:

In a saucepan, melt the butter over medium heat.

Stir in the all-purpose flour to create a roux. Cook for a minute or two until the roux becomes lightly golden.

Gradually whisk in the milk to create a smooth sauce. Continue to cook and stir until the sauce thickens.

Add the grated Pecorino Romano cheese and stir until it's fully melted and the sauce is smooth.

Season the sauce with salt and black pepper to taste. Set the Mornay sauce aside.

2. Assemble the Hot Brown:

Preheat your broiler.

On an oven-safe dish, place the four slices of thick-cut white bread to form the base.

Layer slices of roasted turkey breast over the bread.

Place cooked bacon strips on top of the turkey.

Add sliced tomatoes on top of the bacon.

Pour the prepared Mornay sauce generously over the entire dish.

3. Broil and Garnish:

Place the dish under the broiler and broil until the top is bubbly and golden brown.

Remove from the broiler and garnish the Kentucky Hot Brown with additional Pecorino Romano cheese, a sprinkle of paprika, and fresh parsley.

Tips:

To save time, you can use pre-cooked bacon and pre-sliced roasted turkey breast for convenience.

The Mornay sauce is a classic French sauce made with cheese. It adds a rich and creamy element to the Hot Brown. Be sure to season it to taste.

The traditional garnishes for a Kentucky Hot Brown include Pecorino Romano cheese, paprika, and fresh parsley. These toppings not only add flavor but create a visually appealing dish.

The Kentucky Hot Brown is often served as an open-faced sandwich. You can serve it with a knife and fork, making it a delightful and satisfying meal.

Whether you're serving it for brunch, lunch, or dinner, the Kentucky Hot Brown is a Kentucky tradition that's sure to please your taste buds. Enjoy this classic dish and savor its unique blend of flavors.

2.16 North Carolina: Pulled Pork BBQ

Pulled Pork BBQ

Introduction to the Dish:

North Carolina Pulled Pork BBQ is a classic Southern dish with a rich and flavorful history. It's a barbecue masterpiece, showcasing tender, slow-cooked pork that's been seasoned with a blend of spices, and then pulled apart into succulent shreds. The pork is traditionally served on a soft bun or white bread with a generous drizzle of tangy and spicy vinegar-based BBQ sauce. This iconic dish is a testament to the barbecue traditions of North Carolina and is beloved by barbecue enthusiasts far and wide.

Ingredients:

For the Pork:

- 4-5 pounds of pork shoulder or pork butt
- 2 tablespoons brown sugar
- 2 tablespoons paprika
- 1 tablespoon kosher salt
- 1 tablespoon black pepper
- 1 teaspoon cayenne pepper (adjust to taste)
- 1 teaspoon garlic powder
- 1 teaspoon onion powder
- 1 teaspoon dried thyme (optional)
  - 1/2 teaspoon ground cumin (optional)

Step-by-Step Instructions:

1. Prepare the Pork:

In a small bowl, mix together the brown sugar, paprika, kosher salt, black pepper, cayenne pepper, garlic powder, onion powder, dried thyme, and ground cumin (if using).

Rub the spice mixture generously all over the pork shoulder or pork butt, making sure to coat it evenly. Cover the seasoned pork and refrigerate it for at least a few hours or overnight for the best flavor.

2. Slow Cook the Pork:

Preheat your smoker or grill to 225-250°F (107-121°C) using indirect heat. If using a smoker, you can use wood chips like hickory, applewood, or cherry for added smoky flavor.

Place the seasoned pork on the grill or smoker, and let it cook low and slow for about 6-8 hours, or until the internal temperature reaches around 195-205°F (90-96°C). Keep the

For the Vinegar-based BBQ Sauce:

- 1 cup apple cider vinegar
- 1/2 cup ketchup
- 1/4 cup brown sugar
- 2 tablespoons crushed red pepper flakes
- 1 tablespoon hot sauce (adjust to taste)
- 1 teaspoon kosher salt
- 1/2 teaspoon black pepper
- 1/2 teaspoon garlic powder

For Serving:

- Hamburger buns or white bread
- Coleslaw

temperature consistent and check the pork occasionally to ensure it's cooking evenly.

Once the pork is cooked and tender, remove it from the grill or smoker, and let it rest for about 30 minutes. Then, use two forks to pull the meat into shreds.

3. Prepare the Vinegar-based BBQ Sauce:

In a saucepan, combine the apple cider vinegar, ketchup, brown sugar, crushed red pepper flakes, hot sauce, kosher salt, black pepper, and garlic powder. Heat the sauce over low heat and simmer for about 10 minutes, stirring occasionally.

4. Serve Pulled Pork BBQ:

Serve the pulled pork on hamburger buns or white bread, topped with coleslaw, and generously drizzled with the vinegar-based BBQ sauce.

Tips:

You can use a variety of woods for smoking, each imparting a unique flavor to the pork. Experiment to find your favorite.

Coleslaw is a classic topping for North Carolina Pulled Pork BBQ, providing a cool and crunchy contrast to the smoky and savory pork.

The pork can also be slow-cooked in an oven at a low temperature (around 225-250°F) if you don't have access to a grill or smoker. Use a roasting pan with a lid to help retain moisture.

To balance the spicy and tangy flavors of the BBQ sauce, you can adjust the amount of hot sauce and crushed red pepper flakes to your preferred level of heat.

North Carolina Pulled Pork BBQ is a Southern tradition and a beloved dish at barbecues and gatherings. Enjoy it with family and friends, and savor the taste of authentic Southern barbecue.

2.17 South Carolina: Shrimp and Grits

Shrimp and Grits

Introduction to the Dish:

South Carolina Shrimp and Grits is a beloved Southern classic, known for its delightful combination of creamy, cheesy grits and perfectly cooked shrimp. This dish has its roots in the Lowcountry of South Carolina, where shrimp are plentiful and grits are a staple. The creamy grits serve as a comforting base for the savory, flavorful shrimp and bacon gravy. It's a delicious and hearty dish that beautifully balances the flavors of the sea and the land.

Ingredients:

For the Grits:

- 1 cup stone-ground grits
- 4 cups water
- 1 cup milk
- 2 tablespoons butter
- Salt to taste
- 1 cup shredded cheddar cheese (optional)

For the Shrimp:

- 1 pound large shrimp, peeled and deveined
- 4 slices bacon, chopped
- 1 small onion, finely chopped
- 1 bell pepper, finely chopped

Step-by-Step Instructions:

1. Prepare the Grits:

In a heavy saucepan, bring the water and milk to a boil.

Gradually whisk in the stone-ground grits and reduce the heat to low.

Stir occasionally as the grits cook, which may take 20-30 minutes. Follow the package instructions for your specific grits.

Once the grits are cooked, stir in the butter, salt, and shredded cheddar cheese if desired. Keep the grits warm.

2. Prepare the Shrimp:

In a large skillet, cook the chopped bacon over medium heat until it becomes crispy. Remove the bacon with a slotted spoon and set it aside.

In the same skillet, add the chopped onion and bell pepper. Sauté until they become tender, about 5 minutes.

- 2 cloves garlic, minced
- 1 cup chicken broth
- 1/2 cup heavy cream
- 1/2 cup chopped scallions (green onions)
- 2 tablespoons butter
- 1 tablespoon all-purpose flour
- 1 teaspoon lemon juice
- Salt and black pepper to taste
- Cayenne pepper or hot sauce (optional, for heat)

Add the minced garlic and cook for an additional 30 seconds until fragrant.

In a separate bowl, dust the peeled and deveined shrimp with all-purpose flour to lightly coat them.

Push the sautéed vegetables to one side of the skillet and add the shrimp. Cook the shrimp for 1-2 minutes on each side or until they turn pink.

3. Make the Shrimp Gravy:

Pour in the chicken broth and heavy cream. Stir to combine and let the mixture come to a simmer.

Add the butter and stir until it's melted and the sauce thickens slightly.

Stir in the cooked bacon and chopped scallions. Season with lemon juice, salt, black pepper, and cayenne pepper or hot sauce (if you like it spicy). Adjust the seasoning to your taste.

4. Serve Shrimp and Grits:

To serve, ladle a portion of the creamy grits onto a plate or bowl. Top with the shrimp and shrimp gravy mixture.

Tips:

Stone-ground grits are preferred for their authentic texture and flavor, but you can also use regular grits or instant grits if needed.

The addition of shredded cheddar cheese to the grits provides extra creaminess and flavor. It's optional but highly recommended.

The bacon and the shrimp gravy give this dish its savory richness. Feel free to adjust the level of spiciness with cayenne pepper or hot sauce according to your preference.

South Carolina Shrimp and Grits is a versatile dish that can be served for breakfast, brunch, or dinner. It's a Southern comfort food staple that's sure to please your taste buds. Enjoy the combination of creamy, cheesy grits with perfectly cooked shrimp and savory bacon gravy.

2.18 Georgia: Southern Fried Chicken

Southern Fried Chicken

Introduction to the Dish:

Georgia Southern Fried Chicken is a beloved classic that embodies the essence of Southern comfort food. This iconic dish features tender, juicy chicken pieces with a crispy, golden-brown coating. The secret to its exceptional flavor is marinating the chicken in buttermilk and seasoning it with a blend of spices. When fried to perfection, it offers a satisfying crunch with a burst of savory goodness. Whether it's a Sunday dinner or a picnic, Southern Fried Chicken is a timeless favorite that brings friends and family together.

Ingredients:

- 3-4 pounds of chicken pieces (such as drumsticks, thighs, wings, and breast quarters)
- 2 cups buttermilk
- 2 cups all-purpose flour
- 2 teaspoons salt
- 1 teaspoon black pepper
- 1 teaspoon paprika
- 1/2 teaspoon cayenne pepper (adjust to taste for spiciness)
- 1/2 teaspoon garlic powder
- 1/2 teaspoon onion powder
- Vegetable oil for frying

Step-by-Step Instructions:

1. Marinate the Chicken:

Place the chicken pieces in a large bowl and pour the buttermilk over them. Ensure the chicken is well coated. Marinate in the refrigerator for at least 2 hours, but overnight is even better.

2. Prepare the Breading Mixture:

In a shallow dish, combine the all-purpose flour, salt, black pepper, paprika, cayenne pepper, garlic powder, and onion powder. Mix well to create the breading mixture.

3. Bread the Chicken:

Remove a piece of chicken from the buttermilk, allowing any excess to drip off.

Coat the chicken in the breading mixture, pressing the mixture onto the chicken to ensure an even coating. Place the breaded chicken on a wire rack.

Repeat the process for all chicken pieces. Let them rest for about 15 minutes to allow the coating to set.

4. Heat the Oil:

In a large, deep skillet or Dutch oven, add enough vegetable oil to submerge the chicken pieces. Heat the oil to 350-375°F (177-190°C). Use a candy or deep-fry thermometer for accuracy.

5. Fry the Chicken:

Carefully place a few pieces of breaded chicken into the hot oil, making sure not to overcrowd the skillet. Fry in batches if necessary.

Fry the chicken for about 15-20 minutes, turning occasionally, until it's golden brown and the internal temperature reaches 165°F (74°C). Thicker pieces, like breast quarters, may take a bit longer.

Use a slotted spoon or tongs to transfer the fried chicken to a wire rack or paper towels to drain excess oil.

6. Serve Southern Fried Chicken:

Serve the Southern Fried Chicken while it's hot and crispy. It's delicious on its own or with classic Southern sides like biscuits, coleslaw, or mashed potatoes.

Tips:

Marinating the chicken in buttermilk not only adds flavor but also helps tenderize the meat.

The seasoning in the breading mixture can be adjusted to your taste. If you prefer a spicier chicken, increase the amount of cayenne pepper.

It's important to maintain the oil temperature for even and crispy frying. Use a thermometer to monitor the oil.

Allow the fried chicken to rest on a wire rack to maintain its crispiness. Placing it on paper towels can result in a soggy bottom.

Southern Fried Chicken is a Southern tradition, and the method described above will give you the classic flavor and texture. Enjoy this iconic dish with your favorite sides and savor the taste of the South.

2.19 Florida: Key Lime Pie

Key Lime Pie

Introduction to the Dish:

Florida Key Lime Pie is a delightful and iconic dessert that captures the essence of the Sunshine State. This pie is famous for its sweet and tart key lime filling, which is perfectly complemented by a buttery graham cracker crust. It's a refreshing and tropical treat that's ideal for warm weather or any time you crave a slice of paradise. The balance of zesty citrus and sweet creaminess makes Key Lime Pie a true Floridian delicacy.

Ingredients:

For the Graham Cracker Crust:

- 1 1/2 cups graham cracker crumbs
- 1/4 cup granulated sugar
- 1/2 cup unsalted butter, melted

For the Key Lime Filling:

- 3/4 cup key lime juice (freshly squeezed, if possible)
- 2 teaspoons key lime zest (from about 10-12 key limes)
- 4 large egg yolks
- 1 can (14 ounces) sweetened condensed milk

For the Whipped Cream Topping:

Step-by-Step Instructions:

1. Prepare the Graham Cracker Crust:

Preheat your oven to 350°F (175°C).

In a mixing bowl, combine the graham cracker crumbs and granulated sugar.

Pour the melted butter over the crumb mixture and stir until the crumbs are evenly coated.

Press the mixture firmly into a 9-inch pie dish to form the crust. Use the back of a spoon or the bottom of a measuring cup to ensure a smooth and even crust.

Bake the crust in the preheated oven for about 10 minutes, or until it's set and lightly golden. Allow it to cool while you prepare the filling.

2. Make the Key Lime Filling:

In a separate mixing bowl, whisk together the key lime juice, key lime zest, egg yolks, and sweetened condensed milk until well combined.

Pour the key lime filling into the baked graham cracker crust.

- 1 cup heavy whipping cream
- 2 tablespoons powdered sugar
- 1/2 teaspoon vanilla extract

Bake the pie in the preheated oven for about 15 minutes. The filling should be just set, with a slight jiggle in the center.

Remove the pie from the oven and let it cool to room temperature. Then refrigerate it for at least 3 hours, or until it's fully chilled and set.

3. Prepare the Whipped Cream Topping:

In a mixing bowl, combine the heavy whipping cream, powdered sugar, and vanilla extract.

Whip the cream until it forms stiff peaks.

4. Serve Key Lime Pie:

Before serving, spread the whipped cream over the chilled pie.

For added garnish, you can sprinkle some extra key lime zest on top.

Tips:

Key limes are the traditional choice for this pie, but if you can't find them, regular lime juice and zest can be used as a substitute.

For the best flavor, use freshly squeezed key lime juice. Key limes are smaller and more acidic than regular limes.

It's important not to overbake the pie. The filling should be just set in the center when you remove it from the oven.

Key Lime Pie is at its finest when served well-chilled. The contrast between the cold filling and the buttery crust is part of what makes it so delicious.

Enjoy a taste of Florida with this classic dessert, and savor the tangy-sweet flavors of Key Lime Pie. It's a perfect treat for any occasion, whether you're in the Sunshine State or simply dreaming of a tropical getaway.

2.20 Alabama: Fried Catfish

Fried Catfish

Introduction to the Dish:

Alabama Fried Catfish is a Southern delicacy that's as simple as it is delicious. Catfish fillets are coated in a seasoned mixture of cornmeal and flour, then fried to a crispy, golden perfection. The result is a mouthwatering dish that captures the essence of Southern comfort food. It's a popular choice for a casual family meal or a gathering with friends. The crispy, seasoned crust pairs perfectly with the tender, flaky catfish inside.

Ingredients:

- 4 catfish fillets
- 1 cup buttermilk
- 1 cup cornmeal
- 1/2 cup all-purpose flour
- 1 teaspoon salt
- 1/2 teaspoon black pepper
- 1/2 teaspoon paprika
- 1/4 teaspoon cayenne pepper (adjust to taste)
- Vegetable oil for frying
- Lemon wedges and tartar sauce for serving (optional)

Step-by-Step Instructions:

1. Prepare the Catfish:

In a bowl, place the catfish fillets and pour the buttermilk over them. Ensure the catfish is well coated. Allow it to marinate in the buttermilk for at least 30 minutes, but longer is better.

2. Prepare the Breading Mixture:

In a shallow dish, combine the cornmeal, all-purpose flour, salt, black pepper, paprika, and cayenne pepper. Mix well to create the breading mixture.

3. Bread the Catfish:

Remove a catfish fillet from the buttermilk, letting any excess drip off.

Coat the fillet in the breading mixture, pressing the mixture onto the catfish to ensure an even coating. Place the breaded fillet on a plate or tray. Repeat this process for all the catfish fillets.

4. Heat the Oil:

In a large skillet or deep fryer, add enough vegetable oil to submerge the catfish fillets. Heat the oil to 350-375°F (175-190°C). Use a thermometer to monitor the temperature.

5. Fry the Catfish:

Carefully place one or two breaded catfish fillets into the hot oil. Be cautious not to overcrowd the pan.

Fry the catfish for about 3-4 minutes per side, or until the coating is golden brown and the fish inside is cooked through. The internal temperature of the catfish should reach 145°F (63°C).

Use a slotted spatula or tongs to transfer the fried catfish to a plate lined with paper towels to drain excess oil. Repeat this process for the remaining catfish fillets.

6. Serve Fried Catfish:

Serve the Alabama Fried Catfish while it's hot and crispy. It's traditionally served with lemon wedges and tartar sauce for dipping, but you can also enjoy it with your favorite sides.

Tips:

Marinating the catfish in buttermilk adds flavor and helps tenderize the fish. It also creates a good surface for the breading to adhere to.

The seasoning in the breading mixture can be adjusted to your taste. If you like it spicier, increase the amount of cayenne pepper.

To maintain the crispiness, it's essential to keep the oil temperature consistent throughout the frying process. Use a thermometer to ensure the oil is at the right temperature.

Serve Alabama Fried Catfish with traditional Southern sides like coleslaw, hushpuppies, and collard greens for an authentic Southern meal.

Enjoy the savory, crispy delight of Alabama Fried Catfish, a classic Southern dish that's perfect for any occasion. Whether you're dining at a local Southern restaurant or recreating this dish at home, it's a true Southern comfort food favorite.

CHAPTER
III
Southern U.S

Gumbo

Introduction to the Dish:

Louisiana Gumbo is a rich and flavorful stew that epitomizes the multicultural influences of the region. This iconic Creole and Cajun dish features a dark, flavorful roux, a variety of meats and vegetables, and a combination of spices that create a symphony of taste. Gumbo is often referred to as the "official cuisine" of Louisiana, and it's a dish that brings people together in celebration. Whether you prefer seafood, chicken, or a combination of both, gumbo offers a taste of the vibrant culture and history of the region.

Ingredients:

For the Roux:

- 1/2 cup vegetable oil
- 1/2 cup all-purpose flour

For the Gumbo:

- 1 pound andouille sausage, sliced
- 1 pound boneless, skinless chicken thighs, cut into bite-sized pieces
- 1 large onion, chopped
- 1 green bell pepper, chopped
- 2 celery stalks, chopped
- 4 cloves garlic, minced
- 4 cups chicken broth

Step-by-Step Instructions:

1. Make the Roux:

In a large, heavy-bottomed pot, heat the vegetable oil over medium heat.

Gradually whisk in the all-purpose flour to create the roux. Stir constantly to prevent burning. This process may take about 30-45 minutes, and the roux should become a rich, dark brown color.

2. Prepare the Gumbo:

Add the andouille sausage to the dark roux and cook for about 5 minutes, allowing the sausage to release its flavor.

Stir in the chopped chicken and cook until it's browned.

Add the chopped onion, green bell pepper, and celery. Cook for about 5-7 minutes, or until the vegetables are softened.

Stir in the minced garlic and cook for another minute until fragrant.

- 1 can (14 ounces) diced tomatoes
- 1 cup okra, sliced (fresh or frozen)
- 1 teaspoon dried thyme
- 1 teaspoon dried oregano
- 1/2 teaspoon cayenne pepper (adjust to taste)
- Salt and black pepper to taste
- 2 bay leaves
- Cooked white rice for serving
- Chopped green onions and file powder (optional, for garnish)

Pour in the chicken broth and diced tomatoes, and bring the mixture to a simmer.

Add the sliced okra, dried thyme, dried oregano, cayenne pepper, salt, black pepper, and bay leaves. Stir well.

3. Simmer and Serve:

Reduce the heat to low, cover the pot, and let the gumbo simmer for about 1 to 1.5 hours. Stir occasionally, and remove the bay leaves when done.

4. Serve Gumbo:

Serve the Louisiana Gumbo hot over a bed of cooked white rice.

Optionally, garnish with chopped green onions and a sprinkle of file powder if desired.

Tips:

The roux is the heart of gumbo and requires patience. Stir constantly while making it to avoid burning. If it does burn, you'll need to start over.

Gumbo can be made with a variety of proteins, including shrimp, crab, and even duck. Feel free to personalize it based on your preferences.

File powder, made from sassafras leaves, is a traditional thickening agent. Sprinkle it on the gumbo just before serving.

Gumbo is often even better the next day as the flavors meld, so don't hesitate to make a big batch.

Enjoy this rich and hearty dish that is not only a staple of Louisiana cuisine but also a symbol of Southern hospitality. Whether you're cooking for a special occasion or craving a taste of the South, Louisiana Gumbo is a crowd-pleaser.

3.2 Texas: Chicken Fried Steak

Chicken Fried Steak

Introduction to the Dish:

Texas Chicken Fried Steak is a Southern comfort food classic that features tenderized round steak coated in a seasoned flour mixture and fried to crispy perfection. It's often served with creamy white gravy for a hearty and indulgent meal that's beloved in the Lone Star State and beyond. Chicken Fried Steak is a symbol of Texas hospitality and a dish that satisfies both the soul and the appetite.

Ingredients:

For the Steak:

- 4 cube steaks (tenderized round steak)
- 1 cup all-purpose flour
- 1 teaspoon salt
- 1/2 teaspoon black pepper
- 1/2 teaspoon paprika
- 1/4 teaspoon cayenne pepper (adjust to taste)
- 1/4 teaspoon garlic powder
- 1/4 teaspoon onion powder
- 2 large eggs
- 1/4 cup buttermilk
- Vegetable oil for frying

For the Gravy:

Step-by-Step Instructions:

1. Prepare the Steak:

In a shallow dish, combine the all-purpose flour, salt, black pepper, paprika, cayenne pepper, garlic powder, and onion powder. Mix well.

In another shallow dish, whisk together the eggs and buttermilk.

Dredge each cube steak in the seasoned flour, ensuring it's evenly coated. Shake off any excess.

Dip the coated steak into the egg mixture, allowing any excess to drip off.

Coat the steak once again with the seasoned flour. Press the flour mixture onto the steak to create a thick coating. Place the coated steak on a plate or tray.

2. Fry the Steak:

In a large skillet, add enough vegetable oil to submerge the steaks halfway. Heat the oil to 350-375°F (175-190°C).

- 1/4 cup pan drippings from frying the steak (or vegetable oil)
- 1/4 cup all-purpose flour
- 2 cups milk
- Salt and black pepper to taste

Carefully place the coated steaks into the hot oil, being cautious not to overcrowd the pan. You may need to fry them in batches.

Fry the steaks for about 4-5 minutes per side, or until they are golden brown and cooked through. The internal temperature should reach 160°F (71°C). Transfer the fried steaks to a plate lined with paper towels to drain excess oil.

3. Make the Gravy:

In the same skillet, leave about 1/4 cup of pan drippings (or add vegetable oil if needed).

Sprinkle the 1/4 cup of all-purpose flour into the pan drippings and cook over medium heat. Stir constantly for a few minutes until the mixture turns golden brown.

Gradually pour in the milk while stirring to create a smooth gravy. Continue cooking and stirring until the gravy thickens. Season with salt and black pepper to taste.

4. Serve Chicken Fried Steak:

Serve the hot and crispy Texas Chicken Fried Steak with the creamy white gravy drizzled on top.

Tips:

The cube steak can be purchased pre-tenderized, or you can tenderize it further by using a meat mallet.

Adjust the level of cayenne pepper in the breading to suit your desired level of spiciness.

Serve Chicken Fried Steak with classic sides like mashed potatoes, creamed corn, and green beans for an authentic Southern comfort food experience.

Enjoy the ultimate Southern comfort food with Texas Chicken Fried Steak, a timeless dish that captures the flavors and traditions of the Lone Star State. Whether you're serving it for a family dinner or a special occasion, it's a satisfying and hearty meal.

3.3 Georgia: Peach Cobbler

Peach Cobbler

Introduction to the Dish:

Georgia Peach Cobbler is a classic Southern dessert that showcases the sweetness of ripe peaches in a warm, comforting cobbler. With a golden, biscuit-like topping and a bubbling fruit filling, it's a delightful way to enjoy the flavors of summer all year round. This dessert is often served with a scoop of vanilla ice cream or a dollop of whipped cream, making it an irresistible treat that captures the essence of Georgia's peach-growing heritage.

Ingredients:

For the Filling:

- 4 cups fresh or frozen peaches, peeled, pitted, and sliced (about 4-5 peaches)
- 1 cup granulated sugar
- 1/4 cup brown sugar
- 1/2 teaspoon ground cinnamon
- 1/4 teaspoon ground nutmeg
- 1 teaspoon lemon juice
- 2 tablespoons cornstarch

For the Cobbler Topping:

- 1 cup all-purpose flour
- 1/2 cup granulated sugar
- 1 teaspoon baking powder
- 1/2 teaspoon salt

Step-by-Step Instructions:

1. Prepare the Peach Filling:

Preheat your oven to 350°F (175°C).

In a large bowl, combine the sliced peaches, granulated sugar, brown sugar, ground cinnamon, ground nutmeg, lemon juice, and cornstarch. Toss to coat the peaches evenly.

2. Assemble and Bake:

Transfer the peach mixture into a 9x13-inch baking dish.

In a separate bowl, make the cobbler topping. In that bowl, combine the all-purpose flour, granulated sugar, baking powder, and salt.

Pour in the melted unsalted butter and the hot water. Stir until you have a smooth batter.

Carefully spoon the batter over the peach filling. It doesn't need to cover the peaches completely; the batter will spread and expand as it bakes.

3. Bake the Cobbler:

- 1/2 cup unsalted butter, melted
- 1/4 cup hot water

Place the baking dish in the preheated oven and bake for about 45-50 minutes or until the cobbler topping is golden brown, and the peach filling is bubbling.

4. Serve Peach Cobbler:

Allow the Georgia Peach Cobbler to cool slightly before serving.

Serve warm portions with a scoop of vanilla ice cream or a dollop of whipped cream, if desired.

Tips:

You can use fresh or frozen peaches for this recipe. If using frozen peaches, be sure to thaw and drain them before using.

Adjust the amount of sugar based on the sweetness of your peaches and your personal taste.

To prevent the cobbler topping from becoming too doughy, it's essential to spoon the batter gently over the peaches. It will spread and puff as it bakes.

The cobbler is best enjoyed fresh and warm, but you can reheat it in the oven or microwave if you have leftovers.

Georgia Peach Cobbler is a crowd-pleaser, whether it's at a summer cookout, family gathering, or as a sweet ending to a weeknight dinner. It's a true taste of the South and a delicious way to celebrate the beloved Georgia peach.

3.4 Tennessee: Hot Chicken

Hot Chicken

Introduction to the Dish:

Tennessee Hot Chicken is a fiery and flavorful Southern dish known for its intense spiciness and irresistible flavor. Traditionally, chicken is marinated in buttermilk, coated in a fiery spice blend, and deep-fried to a golden crisp. The chicken is then brushed with a spicy sauce made from the frying oil, resulting in a delicious and spicy meal that's a staple of Nashville cuisine. Served with pickles and white bread, this dish is a true Southern comfort food experience.

Ingredients:

For the Chicken:

- 4 bone-in, skin-on chicken thighs
- 2 cups buttermilk
- 2 cups all-purpose flour
- 2 tablespoons paprika
- 1 tablespoon cayenne pepper (adjust to taste)
- 1 tablespoon brown sugar
- 1 teaspoon garlic powder
- 1 teaspoon salt
- Vegetable oil for frying

For the Spicy Sauce:

- 1/4 cup hot chicken frying oil (from the fried chicken)
- 2 tablespoons cayenne pepper
- 1 tablespoon brown sugar

Step-by-Step Instructions:

1. Marinate the Chicken:

In a large bowl, place the chicken thighs and cover them with buttermilk. Let them marinate in the refrigerator for at least 1 hour, or overnight if possible.

2. Prepare the Spice Blend:

In a separate bowl, mix the all-purpose flour, paprika, cayenne pepper, brown sugar, garlic powder, and salt. This is your spicy flour coating.

3. Coat and Fry the Chicken:

Remove the chicken from the buttermilk and let any excess drip off.

Dip each chicken thigh into the spicy flour coating, ensuring it's well coated.

In a large skillet, heat about 2 inches of vegetable oil over medium-high heat to 350°F (175°C).

Carefully add the coated chicken thighs to the hot oil. Fry for about 15-20 minutes or until the chicken is cooked through and

- 1/2 teaspoon paprika
- 1/2 teaspoon garlic powder
- Salt to taste

For Serving:

- Pickles and white bread

the coating is golden and crisp. Make sure the internal temperature of the chicken reaches 165°F (74°C).

4. Prepare the Spicy Sauce:

In a small saucepan, combine 1/4 cup of the hot chicken frying oil, cayenne pepper, brown sugar, paprika, and garlic powder. Season with salt to taste.

Heat the sauce over low heat, stirring until well combined.

5. Brush the Chicken with Spicy Sauce:

Once the chicken is done frying, remove it from the oil and drain on paper towels.

While the chicken is still hot, brush it generously with the prepared spicy sauce. Be sure to coat both sides.

6. Serve Tennessee Hot Chicken:

Serve the hot chicken with pickles and white bread to help cool down the heat.

Tips:

Adjust the level of cayenne pepper to suit your preferred level of spiciness. Tennessee Hot Chicken is known for its heat, so don't be shy with the spice if you like it hot.

The buttermilk marinade not only imparts flavor but also helps tenderize the chicken.

If you're concerned about the spiciness, you can use less cayenne pepper in the spicy flour coating and the sauce.

Traditional sides for Hot Chicken include coleslaw and pickles to help balance the heat.

Tennessee Hot Chicken is a fiery and delicious dish that's a hallmark of Southern cuisine, particularly in Nashville. Whether you're a fan of spicy food or seeking to experience a true taste of the South, this dish is sure to leave a lasting impression.

3.5 Mississippi: Shrimp and Grits

Shrimp and Grits

Introduction to the Dish:

Mississippi Shrimp and Grits is a Southern classic known for its delightful combination of creamy, cheesy grits and succulent shrimp in a rich, flavorful sauce. This dish embodies the essence of Southern comfort food with a touch of Cajun flair. The creamy grits provide the perfect backdrop for the savory and spicy shrimp, making it a beloved meal for breakfast, brunch, or dinner in Mississippi and beyond.

Ingredients:

For the Grits:

- 1 cup stone-ground grits
- 4 cups water
- 1 cup whole milk
- 4 tablespoons unsalted butter
- Salt and black pepper to taste
- 1 cup sharp cheddar cheese, shredded

For the Shrimp:

- 1 pound large shrimp, peeled and deveined
- 4 slices bacon, chopped
- 1 small onion, finely chopped
- 1 small green bell pepper, finely chopped
- 1 small red bell pepper, finely chopped
- 2 cloves garlic, minced

Step-by-Step Instructions:

1. Prepare the Grits:

In a large saucepan, bring the water to a boil.

Gradually whisk in the stone-ground grits, reduce the heat to low, and simmer, stirring often, for about 20-25 minutes or until the grits are thick and creamy.

Stir in the whole milk, unsalted butter, salt, and black pepper.

Add the shredded sharp cheddar cheese and stir until the cheese is melted and the grits are smooth and creamy. Cover and set aside.

2. Cook the Shrimp:

In a large skillet, cook the chopped bacon over medium-high heat until crispy. Remove the bacon from the skillet and set it aside, leaving the bacon drippings in the skillet.

Add the finely chopped onion, green bell pepper, and red bell pepper to the skillet. Sauté until they become tender, which should take about 5 minutes.

- 1/4 cup chicken broth
- 1/4 cup heavy cream
- 1 tablespoon all-purpose flour
- 1 teaspoon Cajun seasoning
- Salt and black pepper to taste
- Chopped green onions for garnish
- Lemon wedges for garnish

Stir in the minced garlic and cook for an additional minute until fragrant.

Push the vegetables to one side of the skillet and sprinkle the all-purpose flour over the other side. Stir the flour into the bacon drippings to form a roux.

Gradually pour in the chicken broth and heavy cream, stirring until the mixture thickens.

Add the Cajun seasoning and season with salt and black pepper.

Return the cooked bacon to the skillet and add the peeled and deveined shrimp. Cook until the shrimp turn pink and opaque, which should take about 4-5 minutes.

3. Serve Mississippi Shrimp and Grits:

Spoon a generous portion of the creamy cheese grits onto a plate or bowl.

Top the grits with the shrimp and sauce mixture.

Garnish with chopped green onions and serve with lemon wedges.

<u>Tips:</u>

Use stone-ground grits for the best flavor and texture. They take a bit longer to cook but are worth the effort.

Adjust the level of Cajun seasoning to your desired level of spiciness.

The sauce should be rich and flavorful, so don't skip the roux step. It helps thicken the sauce and adds depth of flavor.

Feel free to customize the dish with additional ingredients like sliced mushrooms, diced tomatoes, or even a poached egg on top.

Mississippi Shrimp and Grits is a true Southern comfort food that combines creamy, cheesy grits with spicy, savory shrimp. It's a dish that captures the heart of Mississippi cuisine and is perfect for any meal of the day.

Fried Catfish

Introduction to the Dish:

Alabama Fried Catfish is a beloved Southern dish known for its crispy, golden-brown exterior and tender, flavorful catfish. This classic Southern recipe combines a perfectly seasoned cornmeal coating with the delicious taste of catfish, creating a dish that's cherished across the state of Alabama. Served with lemon wedges and tartar sauce, it's a true Southern delicacy.

Ingredients:

- 4 catfish fillets
- 1 cup cornmeal
- 1/2 cup all-purpose flour
- 1 teaspoon salt
- 1/2 teaspoon black pepper
- 1/2 teaspoon cayenne pepper (adjust to taste)
- 1/2 teaspoon paprika
- 1/2 teaspoon garlic powder
- 1/2 teaspoon onion powder
- Vegetable oil for frying
- Lemon wedges and tartar sauce for serving

Step-by-Step Instructions:

1. Prepare the Catfish:

Rinse the catfish fillets under cold water and pat them dry with paper towels.

Season the fillets with salt and black pepper. Set them aside while you prepare the coating.

2. Create the Coating Mixture:

In a shallow dish, combine the cornmeal, all-purpose flour, salt, black pepper, cayenne pepper, paprika, garlic powder, and onion powder. Mix well to ensure all the spices are evenly distributed.

3. Coat and Fry the Catfish:

Heat vegetable oil in a deep skillet or frying pan to a temperature of 350°F (175°C).

Dip each catfish fillet into the coating mixture, ensuring it's evenly coated on both sides. Press the coating onto the fillets to help it adhere.

Carefully place the coated fillets in the hot oil. Fry them for about 4-5 minutes per side or until they're golden brown and the fish flakes easily with a fork.

Use a slotted spatula to remove the fried catfish from the oil and place them on a plate lined with paper towels to drain any excess oil.

4. Serve Alabama Fried Catfish:

Serve the fried catfish hot with lemon wedges and tartar sauce on the side.

<u>Tips:</u>

Adjust the level of cayenne pepper to suit your preferred level of spiciness. Alabama Fried Catfish can range from mild to moderately spicy, depending on your taste.

For the best results, use catfish fillets that are fresh or thawed from frozen. Pat them dry before seasoning to ensure the coating sticks well.

To ensure a crispy coating, make sure the oil is at the correct temperature (around 350°F or 175°C) before frying the catfish.

It's traditional to serve Alabama Fried Catfish with a side of coleslaw, hushpuppies, or collard greens for a complete Southern meal.

Alabama Fried Catfish is a delightful Southern dish that captures the essence of Alabama cuisine. It's crispy, flavorful, and a perfect example of Southern comfort food.

Lowcountry Boil

Introduction to the Dish:

Lowcountry Boil, also known as Frogmore Stew, is a classic South Carolina dish that embodies the spirit of Southern coastal cuisine. It's a communal, one-pot meal that brings friends and family together. This flavorful boil features a delightful combination of shrimp, smoked sausage, corn, potatoes, and often other seafood like blue crab or crawfish. It's a beloved tradition in the Lowcountry region and throughout South Carolina.

Ingredients:

- 4 quarts water
- 1/2 cup Old Bay Seasoning (adjust to taste)
- 2 pounds large shrimp, unpeeled
- 2 pounds smoked sausage, cut into 2-inch pieces
- 8 ears of corn, shucked and cut into thirds
- 2 pounds small red potatoes
- 2 pounds fresh blue crab (optional)
- 2 pounds crab legs (optional)
- 2 pounds crawfish (optional)
- Lemon wedges and melted butter for serving

Step-by-Step Instructions:

1. Prepare the Cooking Pot:

In a large stockpot or outdoor boiling pot, bring 4 quarts of water to a boil.

Stir in the Old Bay Seasoning. Adjust the amount to your preferred level of spiciness and flavor.

2. Cook the Ingredients:

Start by adding the small red potatoes to the boiling water. Cook for about 10-12 minutes, or until they are almost tender.

Next, add the smoked sausage to the pot and continue cooking for an additional 5 minutes.

Add the corn pieces and continue to cook for another 5 minutes.

If you choose to include blue crab, crab legs, or crawfish, add them to the pot at this point and cook for 5-7 minutes. The crab should turn bright orange, and the crawfish should be bright red.

- Cocktail sauce and hot sauce for dipping

Finally, add the unpeeled shrimp to the pot and cook for 3-5 minutes, or until they turn pink and opaque. Be careful not to overcook the shrimp.

3. Serve Lowcountry Boil:

Once all the ingredients are cooked, carefully drain them in a large colander or directly onto a clean table covered with newspaper.

Spread the Lowcountry Boil out on the table for a fun, communal experience.

Serve with lemon wedges, melted butter, cocktail sauce, and hot sauce on the side.

Tips:

Customize the ingredients to your liking. You can add mussels, clams, or any other seafood you prefer.

Use a large pot for outdoor cooking, and you can even cook this dish over an outdoor burner. It's a popular choice for gatherings and cookouts.

Don't forget to provide plenty of napkins and a bucket for discarding shells.

Lowcountry Boil is best enjoyed outdoors with friends and family. It's a true Southern coastal tradition that brings people together over a delicious, no-fuss meal.

Experiment with the level of spice by adjusting the amount of Old Bay Seasoning to suit your taste.

South Carolina Lowcountry Boil captures the essence of coastal Southern cuisine, making it a popular choice for gatherings and celebrations. It's a flavorful and communal experience that embodies the spirit of the Lowcountry region.

Key Lime Pie

Introduction to the Dish:

Florida Key Lime Pie is a classic and beloved dessert that originated in the Florida Keys. This pie is famous for its sweet and tart flavor, with a creamy and luscious filling nestled in a crisp graham cracker crust. It's a quintessential Florida dessert that captures the essence of the Sunshine State and is perfect for warm, sunny days.

Ingredients:

For the Graham Cracker Crust:

- 1 1/2 cups graham cracker crumbs
- 1/4 cup granulated sugar
- 1/2 cup unsalted butter, melted

For the Key Lime Pie Filling:

- 4 large egg yolks
- 14 ounces (1 can) sweetened condensed milk
- 1/2 cup freshly squeezed key lime juice (regular lime juice can be substituted if key limes are not available)
- Zest of 2 key limes (optional, for extra flavor)
- Whipped cream for garnish

Step-by-Step Instructions:

1. Prepare the Graham Cracker Crust:

Preheat your oven to 350°F (175°C).

In a bowl, combine the graham cracker crumbs, granulated sugar, and melted butter. Mix until the crumbs are evenly coated.

Press the mixture into a 9-inch pie dish, covering the bottom and sides evenly. Use the back of a spoon to press it down firmly.

Bake the crust for about 10 minutes or until it is lightly golden. Remove it from the oven and let it cool while you prepare the filling.

2. Make the Key Lime Pie Filling:

In a bowl, whisk the egg yolks until they are slightly thickened.

Gradually add the sweetened condensed milk and continue to whisk until well combined.

Stir in the key lime juice and zest, if using, and mix until the filling is smooth and well incorporated.

- Key lime slices or zest for garnish (optional)

3. Bake the Pie:

Pour the key lime pie filling into the prepared graham cracker crust.

Bake the pie in the preheated oven for about 15-20 minutes. It should be set but still slightly wobbly in the center.

4. Chill and Serve:

Remove the pie from the oven and let it cool to room temperature.

Refrigerate the pie for at least 2 hours or until it's thoroughly chilled and set.

Before serving, garnish with a dollop of whipped cream and key lime slices or zest, if desired.

Tips:

For the best flavor, try to use fresh key lime juice. Key limes are smaller and more aromatic than regular limes, giving the pie its distinctive taste.

If you can't find key limes, you can use regular lime juice as a substitute.

Be cautious not to overbake the pie. It's done when it's set but still has a slight jiggle in the center.

Feel free to adjust the level of sweetness by adding more or less sweetened condensed milk to suit your taste.

Florida Key Lime Pie is best served chilled, making it a perfect dessert for a hot day. It's a refreshing and delightful taste of Florida's culinary heritage.

3.9 Arkansas: Chicken and Dumplings

Chicken and Dumplings

Introduction to the Dish:

Arkansas Chicken and Dumplings is a hearty and comforting Southern dish that's deeply rooted in the state's culinary traditions. This dish is all about tender pieces of chicken and fluffy dumplings simmered in a rich, flavorful broth. It's the ultimate comfort food, perfect for warming up on a cold day or providing a soothing meal for the soul.

Ingredients:

For the Chicken and Broth:

- 1 whole chicken (about 4 pounds)
- 8 cups water
- 2 celery stalks, chopped
- 2 carrots, chopped
- 1 onion, chopped
- 2 cloves garlic, minced
- Salt and pepper to taste

For the Dumplings:

- 2 cups all-purpose flour
- 1/2 teaspoon salt
- 1/2 teaspoon baking powder
- 2/3 cup milk
- 3 tablespoons unsalted butter, melted

Step-by-Step Instructions:

1. Prepare the Chicken and Broth:

Place the whole chicken in a large stockpot and add 8 cups of water. Make sure the chicken is fully submerged.

Add the chopped celery, carrots, onion, and minced garlic to the pot. Season with salt and pepper to taste.

Bring the mixture to a boil, then reduce the heat to a simmer. Cover and let it simmer for about 1 to 1.5 hours, or until the chicken is fully cooked and tender.

Once the chicken is cooked, remove it from the pot and let it cool. Once it's cool enough to handle, shred the chicken into bite-sized pieces, discarding the skin and bones. Set the shredded chicken aside.

2. Make the Dumplings:

In a mixing bowl, combine the all-purpose flour, salt, and baking powder.

Add the milk and melted butter to the dry ingredients. Stir until the dough comes together. It will be a sticky, thick dough.

On a floured surface, roll the dough out to about 1/8-inch thickness. Use a knife to cut the dough into small squares or rectangles. These will be your dumplings.

3. Simmer the Dumplings:

Return the shredded chicken and the broth to the pot. Bring it to a gentle simmer.

Drop the dumplings into the simmering broth, one at a time, making sure they are submerged. Be careful not to overcrowd the pot. The dumplings will expand as they cook.

Simmer for about 10-15 minutes, or until the dumplings are cooked and no longer doughy in the center.

4. Serve Chicken and Dumplings:

Ladle the chicken and dumplings into bowls, making sure to include a generous amount of the flavorful broth.

<u>**Tips:**</u>

You can add extra vegetables like peas or green beans to the broth for more flavor and color.

Be patient when simmering the dumplings. Let them cook slowly, so they become light and fluffy.

Chicken and Dumplings is all about simplicity and comfort. Feel free to adjust the seasonings to your liking.

This dish is even better the next day as the flavors continue to meld. It's a perfect meal for leftovers.

Serve with a side of freshly baked biscuits or cornbread for a true Southern feast. Enjoy the warmth and comfort of Arkansas Chicken and Dumplings!

3.10 North Carolina: Biscuits and Gravy

Biscuits and Gravy

Introduction to the Dish:

North Carolina Biscuits and Gravy is a classic Southern breakfast dish that's both hearty and satisfying. It's a staple in the South, known for its flaky and tender biscuits smothered in a creamy and savory sausage gravy. This comforting dish is perfect for a leisurely weekend breakfast or brunch.

Ingredients:

For the Biscuits:

- 2 cups all-purpose flour
- 1 tablespoon baking powder
- 1/2 teaspoon salt
- 1/2 cup unsalted butter, cold and cubed
- 3/4 cup milk

For the Gravy:

- 1/2 pound ground pork sausage
- 1/4 cup all-purpose flour
- 2 cups milk
- Salt and black pepper to taste

Step-by-Step Instructions:

1. Make the Biscuits:

Preheat your oven to 450°F (230°C).

In a large mixing bowl, whisk together the all-purpose flour, baking powder, and salt.

Add the cold, cubed butter to the dry ingredients. Use a pastry cutter or your fingers to cut the butter into the flour mixture until it resembles coarse crumbs.

Pour in the milk and stir until the dough just comes together. Be careful not to overmix; it's okay if there are some lumps.

Turn the dough out onto a floured surface and gently knead it a few times. Pat it into a 1-inch thick rectangle.

Use a round biscuit cutter to cut out biscuits. Place them on a baking sheet, with sides touching for soft-sided biscuits or spaced apart for crisp-sided biscuits.

Bake in the preheated oven for about 12-15 minutes or until the biscuits are golden brown.

2. Prepare the Gravy:

While the biscuits are baking, cook the ground pork sausage in a skillet over medium heat, breaking it into crumbles as it cooks. Cook until it's browned and cooked through. Remove any excess grease if needed.

Sprinkle the cooked sausage with all-purpose flour and stir to combine. Cook for a few minutes to eliminate the raw flour taste.

Gradually add the milk to the sausage and flour mixture, stirring continuously to avoid lumps.

Simmer the mixture until it thickens, which should take about 5-7 minutes. Season with salt and black pepper to taste.

3. Serve Biscuits and Gravy:

Split the freshly baked biscuits in half, and spoon the sausage gravy generously over the top.

<u>Tips:</u>

For the best biscuits, use cold butter and handle the dough as little as possible to keep it tender.

If you don't have a biscuit cutter, you can use a round drinking glass to cut out the biscuits.

The sausage gravy should be creamy but not too thick. Adjust the milk to your desired consistency.

Biscuits and Gravy are traditionally a breakfast dish but are also enjoyed as a comfort food for any time of day.

Feel free to add a pinch of cayenne pepper for a bit of heat in the gravy if you like.

Enjoy the comforting flavors of North Carolina Biscuits and Gravy!

3.11 Virginia: Brunswick Stew

Brunswick Stew

Introduction to the Dish:

Virginia Brunswick Stew is a beloved Southern dish with a rich history. This hearty stew is a comforting blend of meats, vegetables, and seasonings. It's often prepared in large batches, making it ideal for gatherings and potlucks. The stew has a slightly smoky and tangy flavor, thanks to the combination of ketchup, barbecue sauce, and vinegar.

Ingredients:

- 2 cups cooked chicken, shredded
- 2 cups cooked pork, shredded
- 2 cups corn kernels (fresh, frozen, or canned)
- 2 cups lima beans (fresh or frozen)
- 2 cups diced tomatoes (canned or fresh)
- 2 cups diced potatoes
- 1 cup diced onion
- 1 cup diced carrots
- 1 cup diced celery
- 1/2 cup ketchup
- 1/4 cup barbecue sauce
- 1/4 cup apple cider vinegar
- 1/4 cup Worcestershire sauce
- 2 tablespoons hot sauce (adjust to taste)
- 2 tablespoons brown sugar
- Salt and black pepper to taste

Step-by-Step Instructions:

1. Prepare the Meats:

Cook the chicken and pork until they are tender and fully cooked. You can use roasted, grilled, or boiled meat. Shred the meat and set it aside.

2. Start the Stew:

In a large stockpot, combine the shredded chicken, shredded pork, corn, lima beans, diced tomatoes, diced potatoes, diced onion, diced carrots, and diced celery.

Add enough water or chicken broth to cover the ingredients.

Stir in the ketchup, barbecue sauce, apple cider vinegar, Worcestershire sauce, hot sauce, brown sugar, salt, and black pepper.

3. Simmer the Stew:

Place the pot over medium heat and bring the mixture to a boil. Once it's boiling, reduce the heat to a simmer.

Allow the stew to simmer, uncovered, for at least 2-3 hours. Stir occasionally, and add more water or chicken broth as needed to keep the stew from becoming too thick. The longer it simmers, the more the flavors meld together.

- Water or chicken broth
  (as needed)

4. Serve Brunswick Stew:

Once the stew is thick and flavorful, it's ready to serve. Taste and adjust the seasoning with more salt, pepper, or hot sauce if desired.

<u>Tips:</u>

Brunswick Stew is traditionally cooked outdoors in large kettles at community gatherings. However, it can be made in a regular kitchen as well.

You can customize the vegetables in the stew to your liking. Some variations include okra, green beans, and bell peppers.

If you're short on time, you can use leftover cooked chicken and pork or even store-bought rotisserie chicken.

Serve the Brunswick Stew with cornbread or crusty bread for a complete meal.

This stew is perfect for making in large batches and freezing for future meals.

Enjoy the comforting flavors of Virginia Brunswick Stew, a Southern classic!

Appalachian Apple Butter

Introduction to the Dish:

West Virginia Appalachian Apple Butter is a delightful and timeless condiment, rich in flavor and tradition. This sweet and spiced apple spread is made by slow-cooking apples with sugar and aromatic spices until it reaches a deep, caramelized, and buttery consistency. It's a staple in Appalachian cuisine, perfect for spreading on biscuits, toast, or using in various recipes.

Ingredients:

- 4-5 pounds of apples (a mix of sweet and tart varieties)
- 4 cups granulated sugar
- 2 teaspoons ground cinnamon
- 1/2 teaspoon ground cloves
- 1/2 teaspoon ground allspice
- 1/2 teaspoon ground nutmeg
- A pinch of salt

Step-by-Step Instructions:

1. Prepare the Apples:

Wash, peel, and core the apples. Cut them into chunks or slices.

2. Cook the Apples:

Place the apple slices in a large, heavy-bottomed pot or slow cooker.

Add the granulated sugar, ground cinnamon, ground cloves, ground allspice, ground nutmeg, and a pinch of salt to the apples. Stir to combine.

Cook the apples and spices over low heat. If you're using a pot, set the heat to low and stir frequently. If using a slow cooker, set it to low or "simmer" and cover.

Simmer the mixture for about 10-12 hours, stirring occasionally, until the apples break down, the mixture darkens, and the consistency thickens. You'll know it's ready when it has the texture of smooth butter.

3. Store the Apple Butter:

While the apple butter is still hot, you can either can it in sterilized jars for long-term storage or store it in airtight containers for shorter use. If canning, follow proper canning procedures.

Tips:

Use a mix of sweet and tart apple varieties for a well-balanced flavor. Apples like Granny Smith, Jonathan, or Fuji work well.

Adjust the sugar and spice levels to your taste. You can make it sweeter or spicier as desired.

Stirring occasionally prevents the mixture from sticking to the pot and ensures even cooking.

You can use a slow cooker to make this apple butter, which is convenient for long, slow cooking.

Apple butter can be used as a spread, a topping for pancakes and waffles, or even as an ingredient in various recipes, such as barbecue sauce or baked goods.

Enjoy the delicious and aromatic West Virginia Appalachian Apple Butter!

3.13 Oklahoma: Okra and Tomatoes

Okra and Tomatoes

Introduction to the Dish:

Oklahoma Okra and Tomatoes is a simple and delicious Southern side dish that showcases the fresh flavors of summer. This dish combines tender okra and ripe tomatoes with aromatic onions and garlic, resulting in a hearty and satisfying medley. It's a classic way to enjoy the bounties of the garden and is perfect as a side dish or served over rice.

Ingredients:

- 1 pound fresh okra, washed and trimmed
- 4 large tomatoes, chopped
- 1 medium onion, finely chopped
- 2 cloves garlic, minced
- 2 tablespoons vegetable oil
- 1/2 teaspoon salt (or to taste)
- 1/4 teaspoon black pepper
- 1/4 teaspoon cayenne pepper (optional, for some heat)
- 1/4 cup fresh cilantro or parsley, chopped (for garnish)

Step-by-Step Instructions:

1. Prepare the Okra:

Wash the okra under cold running water and trim off the tops and tips. You can slice the okra into rounds or leave them whole, depending on your preference.

2. Sauté the Onions and Garlic:

In a large skillet or frying pan, heat the vegetable oil over medium-high heat.

Add the finely chopped onions and sauté for about 3-4 minutes until they become translucent and slightly golden.

Stir in the minced garlic and cook for an additional 30 seconds to 1 minute until fragrant.

3. Cook Okra and Tomatoes:

Add the chopped okra to the skillet and cook for about 5-7 minutes, stirring occasionally. This helps reduce the slime that okra can release.

Once the okra starts to become tender, add the chopped tomatoes to the skillet.

Season with salt, black pepper, and cayenne pepper if you desire a bit of heat. Stir everything together.

4. Simmer:

Reduce the heat to medium-low, cover the skillet, and let the mixture simmer for about 15-20 minutes, or until the okra is tender and the tomatoes have broken down, forming a thick and flavorful sauce.

5. Garnish and Serve:

Just before serving, garnish with fresh cilantro or parsley.

Tips:

The choice of okra and tomatoes is crucial. Fresh, ripe tomatoes and tender okra make all the difference in this dish.

If you want to reduce the slime from okra, you can also soak the okra in vinegar for about 30 minutes before cooking.

Feel free to adjust the seasonings to your taste. If you enjoy spicier dishes, you can add more cayenne pepper or even some chopped jalapeños.

This dish can be served as a side, or you can enjoy it over cooked rice for a more substantial meal.

Leftovers can be stored in the refrigerator and reheated. The flavors tend to meld and become even more delicious over time.

Oklahoma Okra and Tomatoes is a delightful dish that captures the essence of summer in a simple yet flavorful way. Enjoy!

Toasted Ravioli

Introduction to the Dish:

Missouri Toasted Ravioli is a beloved appetizer or snack that hails from St. Louis, Missouri. It consists of cheese-filled ravioli that are breaded, fried until crispy, and typically served with a zesty marinara sauce for dipping. This dish is a delicious combination of textures and flavors, making it a favorite not only in Missouri but throughout the United States.

Ingredients:

For the Ravioli:

1 package of frozen or fresh cheese ravioli
2 cups breadcrumbs
1/2 cup grated Parmesan cheese
2 eggs, beaten
2 tablespoons milk
1/2 teaspoon dried oregano
1/2 teaspoon dried basil
1/2 teaspoon garlic powder
Salt and pepper to taste

For the Marinara Sauce (or use your favorite store-bought sauce):

1 can (28 ounces) crushed tomatoes
2 cloves garlic, minced
1/2 teaspoon dried basil
1/2 teaspoon dried oregano
1/2 teaspoon sugar
Salt and pepper to taste

Step-by-Step Instructions:

1. Bread the Ravioli:

In a bowl, combine the breadcrumbs, grated Parmesan cheese, dried oregano, dried basil, garlic powder, salt, and pepper. Mix well.

In another bowl, whisk together the beaten eggs and milk.

Take each ravioli and dip it into the egg mixture, allowing any excess to drip off.

Next, coat the ravioli in the breadcrumb mixture, pressing gently to ensure the breadcrumbs adhere to the ravioli.

Place the breaded ravioli on a baking sheet lined with parchment paper.

2. Fry the Ravioli:

In a large skillet, heat about 1 inch of vegetable oil over medium-high heat to around 350-375°F (175-190°C).

Carefully add the breaded ravioli to the hot oil in batches, being cautious not to overcrowd the skillet.

Fry the ravioli for about 2-3 minutes on each side, or until they are golden brown and crispy.

Use a slotted spoon to remove the toasted ravioli and place them on a paper towel-lined plate to drain any excess oil.

3. Prepare the Marinara Sauce:

In a separate saucepan, combine the crushed tomatoes, minced garlic, dried basil, dried oregano, sugar, salt, and pepper.

Simmer the sauce over low heat for about 15-20 minutes, stirring occasionally.

4. Serve and Enjoy:

Arrange the toasted ravioli on a serving platter and serve with the marinara sauce for dipping.

Tips:

To save time, you can use store-bought cheese ravioli. However, if you want to make your own, you can use fresh or frozen ravioli.

Make sure the oil is hot enough before frying the ravioli to ensure they become crispy and not overly greasy.

You can experiment with different dipping sauces, like ranch dressing or a creamy garlic sauce.

Serve the toasted ravioli as an appetizer or snack for parties, game day, or any occasion. They are best enjoyed hot and crispy!

Missouri Toasted Ravioli is a delightful and crowd-pleasing dish that's sure to be a hit at any gathering. Enjoy!

Jambalaya

Introduction to the Dish:

Louisiana Jambalaya is a flavorful and hearty one-pot dish that's a true Cajun and Creole classic. It's a melting pot of flavors and cultures, with influences from African, Spanish, and French cuisines. Jambalaya is known for its bold and spicy taste, thanks to the use of Andouille sausage, a variety of seasonings, and the "holy trinity" of vegetables—onions, bell peppers, and celery.

Ingredients:

- 1 pound (450g) Andouille sausage or smoked sausage, sliced
- 1 pound (450g) boneless chicken thighs, cut into bite-sized pieces
- 1 pound (450g) large shrimp, peeled and deveined
- 1 onion, diced
- 1 bell pepper, diced
- 2 celery stalks, diced
- 3 cloves garlic, minced
- 1 can (14.5 ounces) diced tomatoes
- 2 cups long-grain white rice
- 4 cups chicken broth
- 1 teaspoon dried thyme
- 1 teaspoon dried oregano
- 1 teaspoon paprika
- 1/2 teaspoon cayenne pepper (adjust to taste)
- Salt and black pepper to taste

Step-by-Step Instructions:

1. Sear the Meats:

Heat the vegetable oil in a large, heavy-bottomed pot or Dutch oven over medium-high heat.

Add the Andouille sausage slices and cook until they are browned and have released some of their flavorful oils. Remove them and set them aside.

In the same pot, add the diced chicken pieces. Cook until they are browned on all sides. Remove the chicken and set it aside.

2. Sauté the Vegetables:

In the same pot, add the diced onions, bell pepper, and celery. Sauté them until they become softened and translucent, about 5-7 minutes.

Add the minced garlic and sauté for another 1-2 minutes until fragrant.

3. Add Seasonings and Rice:

Stir in the dried thyme, dried oregano, paprika, cayenne pepper, salt, and black pepper.

- 2 tablespoons vegetable oil
- Green onions, chopped (for garnish)

Add the diced tomatoes (with their juice) and rice. Mix well to combine all the ingredients.

4. Simmer and Cook:

Return the cooked sausage and chicken to the pot. Mix everything together.

Pour in the chicken broth and bring the mixture to a boil.

Reduce the heat to low, cover the pot, and let it simmer for about 20-25 minutes, or until the rice is cooked and the liquid is absorbed. Stir occasionally to prevent sticking.

5. Add Shrimp and Finish:

Gently stir in the peeled and deveined shrimp.

Cover the pot and cook for an additional 5-7 minutes, or until the shrimp turn pink and are cooked through.

6. Serve and Garnish:

Remove the pot from heat and let it sit, covered, for a few minutes before serving.

Serve the jambalaya in bowls, garnished with chopped green onions.

Tips:

Adjust the level of spiciness by varying the amount of cayenne pepper to suit your taste.

Jambalaya is incredibly versatile. You can add other proteins like crawfish, crab, or even duck, depending on your preferences and what's available.

Traditional Louisiana Jambalaya often includes okra, but feel free to omit it if you're not a fan or if it's not in season.

Jambalaya is a great make-ahead dish and even tastes better the next day after the flavors have had a chance to meld.

Louisiana Jambalaya is a bold and comforting dish that captures the essence of Creole and Cajun cuisine. Enjoy the rich flavors and spices in every bite!

3.16 Texas: Chicken and Dumplings

Chicken and Dumplings

Texas Chicken and Dumplings is a hearty and comforting dish that warms the soul. It's a classic Southern recipe that's perfect for chilly evenings or when you need a bit of culinary comfort. This dish consists of tender chicken and fluffy dumplings in a savory broth, seasoned with aromatic vegetables and herbs.

Ingredients:

For the Chicken and Broth:

- 1 whole chicken, about 3-4 pounds
- 1 onion, peeled and halved
- 2 carrots, peeled and halved
- 2 celery stalks, halved
- 2 bay leaves
- 8 cups of water
- Salt and pepper to taste

For the Dumplings:

- 2 cups all-purpose flour
- 1 tablespoon baking powder
- 1 teaspoon salt
- 1 cup milk

Step-by-Step Instructions:

1. Cook the Chicken and Make the Broth:

Place the whole chicken in a large pot and add the halved onion, carrots, celery, bay leaves, and water. Season with salt and pepper.

Bring the water to a boil and then reduce the heat to a simmer. Cover and cook for about 1.5 to 2 hours or until the chicken is fully cooked and tender. Skim off any foam that rises to the surface.

Once the chicken is cooked, remove it from the pot and let it cool. Shred the meat and discard the skin and bones. Strain the broth to remove any solids. Set aside both the shredded chicken and the broth.

2. Prepare the Dumplings:

In a mixing bowl, combine the all-purpose flour, baking powder, and salt for the dumplings.

Gradually add the milk, stirring until you have a thick, sticky dough.

For the Soup:

- 2 tablespoons butter
- 1 onion, finely chopped
- 3 carrots, peeled and sliced
- 3 celery stalks, sliced
- 3 cloves garlic, minced
- 1/2 teaspoon dried thyme
- 1/2 teaspoon dried rosemary
- 1/2 cup frozen peas
- Salt and pepper to taste
- Chopped fresh parsley for garnish

3. Cook the Soup:

In a separate large pot, melt the butter over medium heat.

Add the finely chopped onion, sliced carrots, and celery. Sauté until the vegetables are tender, about 5-7 minutes.

Add the minced garlic, dried thyme, and dried rosemary. Cook for an additional 1-2 minutes until fragrant.

Pour in the reserved chicken broth. Bring it to a simmer.

Add the shredded chicken and frozen peas. Season with salt and pepper to taste. Simmer for about 10-15 minutes to meld the flavors.

4. Add the Dumplings:

Drop spoonfuls of the dumpling dough into the simmering broth and chicken mixture. Make sure to evenly distribute the dumplings.

Cover the pot and let it simmer for about 15-20 minutes or until the dumplings are cooked through and no longer doughy.

5. Serve and Garnish:

Ladle the Texas Chicken and Dumplings into bowls.

Garnish with chopped fresh parsley for a pop of color and freshness.

<u>**Tips:**</u>

You can customize the dumplings by adding fresh herbs, such as chopped chives or parsley, to the dough for extra flavor.

Adjust the thickness of the soup by adding more or less milk to the dumpling dough.

If you prefer a thicker broth, you can mix a small amount of cornstarch with water and stir it into the soup. Simmer until it thickens to your liking.

Texas Chicken and Dumplings is even better when reheated the next day as the flavors have had time to meld.

3.17 Alabama: Biscuits and Sausage Gravy

Biscuits and Sausage Gravy

Introduction to the Dish:

Alabama Biscuits and Sausage Gravy is a beloved Southern breakfast classic known for its hearty and flavorful combination of flaky biscuits and creamy sausage gravy. It's a satisfying and comforting meal that's perfect for starting your day with a warm and filling dish.

Ingredients:

For the Biscuits:

- 2 cups all-purpose flour
- 1 tablespoon baking powder
- 1/2 teaspoon salt
- 1/2 cup cold unsalted butter, cubed
- 3/4 cup buttermilk

For the Sausage Gravy:

- 1 pound ground breakfast sausage
- 1/4 cup all-purpose flour
- 2 cups whole milk
- Salt and black pepper to taste
- A pinch of red pepper flakes (optional)

Step-by-Step Instructions:

1. Prepare the Biscuits:

Preheat your oven to 450°F (230°C).

In a large mixing bowl, whisk together the all-purpose flour, baking powder, and salt.

Add the cold, cubed butter to the dry ingredients. Using a pastry cutter or your fingers, work the butter into the flour mixture until it resembles coarse crumbs.

Pour in the buttermilk and stir until just combined. Be careful not to overmix; the dough should be slightly sticky.

Turn the dough out onto a floured surface and gently knead it a few times. Pat it down to about 1/2-inch thickness.

Use a round biscuit cutter or a drinking glass to cut out biscuits. Place the biscuits on an ungreased baking sheet, making sure they touch slightly for soft sides or slightly apart for crisp sides.

Bake for 10-12 minutes or until the biscuits are golden brown on top.

2. Cook the Sausage Gravy:

While the biscuits are baking, cook the ground breakfast sausage in a large skillet over medium-high heat. Use a wooden spoon to break the sausage into small pieces as it cooks.

Once the sausage is browned and cooked through, sprinkle the flour over it. Stir well to coat the sausage with the flour.

Gradually pour in the milk, stirring constantly. Continue cooking and stirring until the mixture thickens and comes to a simmer.

Season the gravy with salt, black pepper, and a pinch of red pepper flakes (if you like a little heat). Adjust the seasoning to your taste.

3. Assemble and Serve:

Split the freshly baked biscuits in half.

Ladle a generous amount of sausage gravy over each biscuit half.

Serve immediately, and enjoy your delicious Alabama Biscuits and Sausage Gravy!

Tips:

Make sure your butter is cold when making the biscuit dough. Cold butter helps create flaky biscuits.

Handle the biscuit dough gently and as little as possible to prevent overmixing, which can make the biscuits tough.

The sausage gravy should be creamy and smooth. If it's too thick, you can add a little more milk to achieve the desired consistency.

Adjust the level of spiciness in the gravy by adding more or fewer red pepper flakes.

Biscuits and Sausage Gravy are often served for breakfast, but they make a hearty brunch or even a comfort food dinner.

Bourbon-Glazed Ham

Introduction to the Dish:

Kentucky Bourbon-Glazed Ham is a delicious and flavorful dish that's perfect for special occasions and holidays. The combination of a succulent ham with a sweet and slightly smoky bourbon glaze creates a memorable centerpiece for your table.

Ingredients:

- 1 bone-in ham (8-10 pounds)
- 1 cup brown sugar
- 1/2 cup bourbon
- 1/4 cup Dijon mustard
- 1/4 cup apple cider vinegar
- 1/4 cup molasses
- 1/4 cup honey
- 1/2 teaspoon ground cloves
- 1/2 teaspoon ground cinnamon
- 1/2 teaspoon ground nutmeg

Step-by-Step Instructions:

1. Prepare the Ham:

Preheat your oven to 325°F (165°C).

Place the ham in a large roasting pan, flat side down. If your ham has skin on it, remove the skin, leaving a layer of fat.

Score the ham by making diagonal cuts about 1 inch apart, creating a diamond pattern on the surface.

2. Prepare the Glaze:

In a saucepan, combine the brown sugar, bourbon, Dijon mustard, apple cider vinegar, molasses, honey, ground cloves, ground cinnamon, and ground nutmeg.

Cook the glaze over medium heat, stirring constantly, until the sugar has dissolved and the mixture thickens slightly. This will take about 5-7 minutes.

3. Glaze the Ham:

Brush a generous amount of the glaze over the ham, making sure to get it into the cuts you made during scoring.

Cover the ham with aluminum foil and place it in the preheated oven.

4. Bake the Ham:

Bake the ham for about 10-15 minutes per pound. The internal temperature should reach 140°F (60°C). Baste the ham with the glaze every 20-30 minutes.

5. Finish and Serve:

During the last 10-15 minutes of baking, remove the foil to allow the ham to caramelize and develop a beautiful, golden crust.

Once the ham reaches the desired temperature and has a lovely glaze, remove it from the oven.

Allow the ham to rest for about 15-20 minutes before carving. This allows the juices to redistribute, keeping the meat moist.

Carve the ham and serve it with any remaining glaze on the side.

Tips:

Choose a high-quality ham for the best results. A bone-in ham will have more flavor and tenderness.

If you're concerned about the alcohol content in the glaze, the bourbon will mostly evaporate during cooking, leaving the flavor without the alcohol.

When basting, be generous with the glaze to ensure a flavorful and shiny finish.

Leftover glazed ham is great for sandwiches, so be sure to save some for the next day.

3.19 Tennessee: Cornbread and Collard Greens

Cornbread and Collard Greens

Introduction to the Dish:

Tennessee Cornbread and Collard Greens is a classic Southern dish that embodies the rich, comforting flavors of the region. Collard greens are slowly simmered with smoky ham hocks or turkey legs, resulting in tender and flavorful greens, while the cornbread complements the dish with its sweet and savory taste.

Ingredients:

For Collard Greens:

- 1 bunch of fresh collard greens
- 6 cups chicken or vegetable broth
- 1 onion, chopped
- 2 cloves garlic, minced
- 1-2 smoked ham hocks or turkey legs (optional)
- 2 tablespoons apple cider vinegar
- Salt and black pepper to taste
- Red pepper flakes (optional, for heat)

For Cornbread:

- 1 cup cornmeal
- 1 cup all-purpose flour
- 1/4 cup granulated sugar

Step-by-Step Instructions:

For Collard Greens:

Start by washing the collard greens thoroughly. Remove the tough stems and chop the leaves into bite-sized pieces.

In a large pot, sauté the chopped onion and minced garlic in a little oil until they become translucent.

Add the smoked ham hocks or turkey legs to the pot. These will infuse the greens with a smoky flavor. If you prefer a vegetarian version, you can omit the meat.

Pour in the chicken or vegetable broth and bring it to a boil.

Add the collard greens to the pot, a handful at a time, allowing them to wilt before adding more. Stir them into the broth.

Season with salt, black pepper, and red pepper flakes for some heat. You can adjust the seasoning to your taste.

Reduce the heat to low, cover the pot, and let the collard greens simmer for at least an hour, or until they are tender and flavorful. Stir occasionally.

Just before serving, add apple cider vinegar for a touch of acidity.

- 1 tablespoon baking powder
- 1/2 teaspoon salt
- 1 cup buttermilk
- 1/3 cup vegetable oil
- 2 large eggs

For Cornbread:

Preheat your oven to 425°F (220°C) and grease an 8-inch square baking pan.

In a mixing bowl, combine the cornmeal, all-purpose flour, granulated sugar, baking powder, and salt.

In a separate bowl, whisk together the buttermilk, vegetable oil, and eggs.

Pour the wet ingredients into the dry ingredients and stir until just combined. Do not overmix; lumps are okay.

Pour the cornbread batter into the prepared pan and smooth the top.

Bake in the preheated oven for 20-25 minutes or until the cornbread is golden brown and a toothpick inserted into the center comes out clean.

Let the cornbread cool for a few minutes before slicing.

Tips:

Collard greens can be quite tough, so be patient when simmering them to achieve the desired tenderness.

If you prefer a vegetarian version, you can use vegetable broth and omit the meat, or use smoked paprika for a smoky flavor.

Serve the cornbread with a pat of butter and honey for a sweet and savory contrast.

Leftover collard greens and cornbread are even better the next day, so don't be afraid to make extra.

CHAPTER IV
Northern U.S

4.1 New York: Buffalo Wings

New York Buffalo Wings

Introduction to the Dish:

New York Buffalo Wings are a beloved American classic, known for their spicy and tangy flavor. These crispy fried chicken wings are coated in a zesty Buffalo sauce that combines the heat of hot sauce with the richness of butter. They are perfect as a game-day snack or a tasty appetizer.

Ingredients:

For the Wings:

- 2 pounds chicken wings, separated into drumettes and flats
- 1 cup all-purpose flour
- 1 teaspoon paprika
- 1 teaspoon garlic powder
- 1/2 teaspoon cayenne pepper (adjust to your heat preference)
- Salt and black pepper to taste
- Vegetable oil for frying

For the Buffalo Sauce:

- 1/2 cup hot sauce (such as Frank's RedHot)
- 1/2 cup unsalted butter
- 1 tablespoon white vinegar
- 1/4 teaspoon garlic powder
- A pinch of salt

Step-by-Step Instructions:

For the Wings:

In a mixing bowl, combine the flour, paprika, garlic powder, cayenne pepper, salt, and black pepper.

Toss the chicken wing pieces in the seasoned flour mixture, making sure they are evenly coated.

Heat the vegetable oil in a deep fryer or a large, deep skillet to 375°F (190°C).

Carefully add the coated chicken wing pieces to the hot oil, ensuring not to overcrowd the pan. Fry in batches if necessary.

Fry the wings for about 10-12 minutes, or until they are golden brown and crispy. The internal temperature should reach 165°F (74°C). Drain on a paper towel-lined plate.

For the Buffalo Sauce:

In a saucepan, melt the unsalted butter over low heat.

Stir in the hot sauce, white vinegar, garlic powder, and a pinch of salt. Adjust the sauce's heat by adding more or less hot sauce to suit your preference.

Once the sauce is well mixed and heated, remove it from the heat.

Assembly:

Place the fried chicken wings in a large mixing bowl.

Pour the Buffalo sauce over the wings and toss them until they are evenly coated.

Tips:

Serve your Buffalo wings with celery sticks and a side of blue cheese dressing for a classic Buffalo wing experience.

Adjust the cayenne pepper in the flour mixture to control the spiciness of the wings.

You can bake the wings instead of frying for a healthier option. Place the coated wings on a baking sheet, and bake at 425°F (220°C) for about 45-50 minutes, turning them halfway through. Then, toss them in the Buffalo sauce.

For extra crispy wings, double fry them. After the initial frying, let them cool for a few minutes, then fry them again for 5-7 minutes until they reach your desired level of crispiness.

4.2 Maine: Lobster Mac and Cheese

Lobster Mac and Cheese

Introduction to the Dish:

Maine Lobster Mac and Cheese is a decadent and rich comfort food dish that combines the creamy goodness of mac and cheese with the luxurious taste of lobster. It's a delightful seafood twist on a classic dish, perfect for special occasions or whenever you want to treat yourself.

Ingredients:

For the Mac and Cheese:

- 8 ounces elbow macaroni
- 4 cups shredded sharp cheddar cheese
- 2 cups shredded Gruyère cheese
- 2 cups whole milk
- 1 cup heavy cream
- 1/2 cup unsalted butter
- 1/2 cup all-purpose flour
- 1/2 teaspoon salt
- 1/4 teaspoon black pepper
- 1/4 teaspoon paprika
- 1/4 teaspoon cayenne pepper (optional)
- 2 cups cooked lobster meat, chopped (about 2 small lobsters)

For the Topping:

- 1/2 cup breadcrumbs

Step-by-Step Instructions:

For the Mac and Cheese:

Cook the elbow macaroni according to the package instructions. Drain and set aside.

In a large pot, melt the 1/2 cup of butter over medium heat. Stir in the flour and cook for about 1-2 minutes, stirring constantly until it forms a smooth paste (a roux).

Gradually whisk in the milk and heavy cream, and continue to cook, whisking constantly, until the mixture thickens, about 5-7 minutes.

Reduce the heat to low and add the shredded cheddar and Gruyère cheese, stirring until the cheese is melted and the sauce is smooth.

Season the cheese sauce with salt, black pepper, paprika, and cayenne pepper if using. Adjust the seasonings to your taste.

Add the cooked macaroni and chopped lobster meat to the cheese sauce, stirring until everything is well combined.

For the Topping:

- 2 tablespoons melted butter
- 1/4 cup grated Parmesan cheese

In a small bowl, combine the breadcrumbs, melted butter, and grated Parmesan cheese.

Assembly:

Preheat your oven to 375°F (190°C).

Transfer the lobster mac and cheese mixture to a greased baking dish.

Sprinkle the breadcrumb topping evenly over the mac and cheese.

Bake in the preheated oven for about 20-25 minutes, or until the topping is golden brown and the mac and cheese is bubbling.

Tips:

When cooking lobster for this dish, you can boil or steam the lobsters, then remove the meat from the shells and chop it into bite-sized pieces.

If you prefer a crustier topping, you can broil the mac and cheese for the last 1-2 minutes of baking, but be sure to watch it closely to avoid burning.

You can add a touch of fresh herbs like chopped chives or parsley for extra flavor and a pop of color.

Serve Maine Lobster Mac and Cheese as a main course for a special dinner or as a delightful side dish at gatherings and celebrations.

New England Clam Chowder

Introduction to the Dish:

New England Clam Chowder is a creamy, hearty soup that's a classic of Massachusetts and the New England region. It's known for its rich flavor, tender clams, and comforting creaminess. Perfect for a chilly day, this chowder will warm your heart and soul.

Ingredients:

- 4 slices of bacon, chopped
- 1 large onion, finely chopped
- 2 stalks celery, finely chopped
- 2 cloves garlic, minced
- 3 cups peeled and diced potatoes
- 1 cup water
- 3 (6.5 oz) cans chopped clams, juice reserved
- 1 cup clam juice (from cans)
- 2 cups whole milk
- 2 cups heavy cream
- 1/4 cup all-purpose flour
- 2 bay leaves
- 1/2 teaspoon dried thyme
- Salt and black pepper to taste
- Chopped fresh parsley for garnish

Step-by-Step Instructions:

In a large soup pot, cook the chopped bacon over medium heat until it's crisp. Remove the bacon and set it aside, leaving about 2 tablespoons of bacon fat in the pot.

Add the chopped onion and celery to the pot with the bacon fat. Sauté them over medium heat until they become translucent and tender, about 5-7 minutes.

Stir in the minced garlic and cook for another 1-2 minutes until fragrant.

Add the diced potatoes to the pot and pour in 1 cup of water. Cook the potatoes until they are fork-tender, usually around 10-15 minutes.

While the potatoes are cooking, in a separate saucepan, combine the reserved clam juice, clam juice from the cans, milk, and heavy cream. Warm this mixture over low heat, but do not boil.

Once the potatoes are tender, gradually whisk in the flour until well combined with the bacon and vegetables. Cook for another 2-3 minutes to remove the raw flour taste.

- Oyster crackers or saltines (optional, for serving)

Slowly pour the warm milk and clam juice mixture into the soup pot while whisking continuously. This will help prevent lumps from forming. Add the bay leaves and dried thyme. Season with salt and black pepper to taste.

Continue cooking the chowder over medium heat, stirring frequently, until it thickens to your desired consistency. This usually takes about 10-15 minutes.

Add the chopped clams and reserved bacon to the chowder. Cook for another 2-3 minutes until the clams are heated through.

Tips:

Serve your New England Clam Chowder with chopped fresh parsley as a garnish. It adds a pop of color and freshness to the dish.

For added authenticity, serve the chowder with oyster crackers or saltines on the side. These can be crumbled into the soup for extra texture.

Adjust the thickness of the chowder by adding more or less flour. You can also adjust the seasoning to suit your taste.

New England Clam Chowder is traditionally served in a bread bowl, but it's just as delicious in a regular bowl.

Be cautious with the salt since clam juice and bacon can already be salty. Taste and adjust before serving.

4.4 Pennsylvania: Pierogies

Pierogies

<u>Introduction to the Dish:</u>

Pierogies are a beloved comfort food that has found a special place in the hearts of Pennsylvanians. These delicious dumplings consist of a tender dough filled with creamy mashed potatoes, cheese, and onions. Whether you enjoy them as a snack, a side dish, or a main course, pierogies are a taste of Pennsylvania's culinary heritage.

<u>Ingredients:</u>

For the Dough:

- 2 cups all-purpose flour
- 1/2 teaspoon salt
- 1 large egg
- 1/2 cup sour cream
- 1/4 cup unsalted butter, softened
- 1/2 cup warm water

For the Filling:

- 2 cups mashed potatoes (prepared with butter and cream)
- 1 cup grated cheddar cheese
- 1 small onion, finely chopped
- Salt and pepper to taste

For Serving:

- Sour cream
- Sauteed onions in butter

<u>Step-by-Step Instructions:</u>

For the Dough:

In a large mixing bowl, combine the flour and salt.

In a separate bowl, whisk together the egg, sour cream, and softened butter.

Pour the wet mixture into the dry ingredients and stir until a shaggy dough forms.

Gradually add the warm water and knead the dough until it's smooth and elastic. You can do this in the bowl or on a floured surface.

Cover the dough with a clean kitchen towel and let it rest for about 30 minutes.

For the Filling:

Prepare mashed potatoes as you normally would, mixing in butter and cream for a creamy consistency. Season with salt and pepper to taste.

In a separate bowl, combine the mashed potatoes, grated cheddar cheese, and finely chopped onions.

Assembling the Pierogies:

Roll out the rested dough on a floured surface to about 1/8-inch thickness.

Use a round cookie cutter or a drinking glass to cut out circles from the dough.

Place a small amount of the potato filling in the center of each dough circle.

Fold the dough over the filling to create a half-moon shape. Seal the edges by pressing with your fingers or a fork.

Cooking the Pierogies:

Bring a large pot of salted water to a boil.

Carefully drop the pierogies into the boiling water and cook until they float to the surface, usually about 3-5 minutes.

Remove the pierogies with a slotted spoon and place them on a plate.

If desired, sauté chopped onions in butter until they are soft and slightly caramelized. Drizzle this mixture over the cooked pierogies.

Tips:

You can get creative with pierogi fillings. Traditional options include cheese and potato, but you can also fill them with sauerkraut, mushrooms, or even sweet fillings like blueberries for a dessert variation.

When folding the pierogies, make sure to seal the edges tightly to prevent the filling from spilling out during cooking.

Leftover pierogies can be reheated by pan-frying them in butter until they are crispy and golden.

Serve pierogies with a dollop of sour cream for a classic and delicious topping.

Some people enjoy pierogies with applesauce as a sweet twist to this savory dish.

4.5 New Jersey: Taylor Ham, Egg, and Cheese Sandwich

Taylor Ham, Egg, and Cheese Sandwich

Introduction to the Dish:

The Taylor Ham, Egg, and Cheese Sandwich, also known as the Pork Roll, Egg, and Cheese Sandwich, is a quintessential breakfast sandwich popular in New Jersey. This delicious creation features thinly sliced and pan-fried Taylor Ham, a round and flavorful processed pork product. It's often paired with eggs and American cheese, served on a bagel, roll, or bread. This sandwich is a beloved morning ritual for many New Jerseyans.

Ingredients:

- Taylor Ham (also known as pork roll)
- Eggs
- American cheese
- Salt and pepper to taste
- Butter or oil for cooking
- Bagels, rolls, or bread for serving

Step-by-Step Instructions:

Prepare the Taylor Ham:

Slice the Taylor Ham into thin rounds. Some people prefer to make small slits around the edges to prevent it from curling when cooked.

In a hot skillet, cook the Taylor Ham slices over medium-high heat until they're slightly crispy and golden brown on both sides. Remove and set them aside.

Cook the Eggs:

In the same skillet, reduce the heat to medium.

Crack eggs into the skillet, season with a pinch of salt and pepper, and cook to your preferred doneness. Many people like the yolks runny, but you can cook them to your liking.

Assemble the Sandwich:

Cut your choice of bread (bagel, roll, or bread) in half and toast it if desired.

Place a slice of American cheese on the bottom half of the bread, followed by the cooked Taylor Ham and eggs.

Optional Additions:

Customize your sandwich with additional toppings like ketchup, hot sauce, or even a hash brown patty for extra flavor and texture.

Cover and Serve:

Place the top half of the bread on the sandwich to create a perfect breakfast package.

Tips:

Taylor Ham can be found in most grocery stores in New Jersey and some parts of the surrounding region. If it's not available in your area, you can order it online or substitute it with another type of breakfast meat like bacon or sausage.

Feel free to get creative with the cheese. While American cheese is traditional, you can use cheddar, Swiss, or any other cheese you prefer.

The choice of bread can vary, too. Many locals love it on a bagel, but kaiser rolls or plain bread work just as well.

Experiment with condiments and toppings to suit your taste. Some people enjoy adding a touch of mustard or even a fried egg to take the sandwich to the next level.

This sandwich is incredibly popular at local diners and eateries, but it's just as easy to make at home. Enjoy it for breakfast or any time you're craving a satisfying meal.

4.6 Vermont: Vermont Maple Syrup Pancakes

Vermont Maple Syrup Pancakes

Introduction to the Dish:

Vermont is renowned for its high-quality maple syrup, and there's no better way to enjoy it than by drizzling it over a stack of light and fluffy Vermont Maple Syrup Pancakes. These pancakes are a delightful breakfast treat that captures the essence of the Green Mountain State. Made with locally sourced ingredients, they are perfect for a cozy weekend morning or a special occasion.

Ingredients:

For the Pancakes:

- 1 cup all-purpose flour
- 2 tablespoons granulated sugar
- 1 teaspoon baking powder
- 1/2 teaspoon baking soda
- 1/4 teaspoon salt
- 1 cup buttermilk
- 1 large egg
- 2 tablespoons unsalted butter, melted
- Cooking spray or additional butter for the griddle

For the Topping:

- Vermont pure maple syrup

Step-by-Step Instructions:

For the Pancakes:

Preheat the Griddle:

Heat a griddle or non-stick skillet over medium-high heat. Lightly grease it with cooking spray or a small amount of butter.

Combine Dry Ingredients:

In a mixing bowl, whisk together the flour, sugar, baking powder, baking soda, and salt.

Mix the Wet Ingredients:

In a separate bowl, beat the buttermilk and egg until well combined.

Add the melted butter to the wet ingredients and mix thoroughly.

Combine Wet and Dry Mixtures:

- Butter

Pour the wet mixture into the dry mixture and stir until just combined. Be careful not to overmix; a few lumps are okay.

Cook the Pancakes:

Ladle 1/4 cup of batter onto the hot griddle for each pancake.

Cook until you see bubbles forming on the surface and the edges appear set. This typically takes 2-3 minutes.

Flip the pancakes and cook for another 2-3 minutes or until they are golden brown and cooked through.

For the Topping:

Serve with Maple Syrup:

Stack the pancakes on a plate, placing a small pat of butter between each.

Pour warm Vermont pure maple syrup generously over the stack.

<u>Tips:</u>

Vermont pure maple syrup is the key to authentic flavor. Be sure to use the real thing, as it enhances the taste and aroma of these pancakes.

To keep the pancakes warm as you cook batches, place them on a baking sheet in a 200°F (93°C) oven.

For a twist, you can add your choice of ingredients to the batter, such as blueberries, chocolate chips, or chopped nuts.

If you don't have buttermilk, you can make a substitute by adding 1 tablespoon of white vinegar or lemon juice to a cup of milk. Stir and let it sit for a few minutes until it thickens.

Maple syrup tends to thicken when cooled. To reheat it and restore its original consistency, simply place the container in a bowl of warm water or microwave it for a few seconds.

These Vermont Maple Syrup Pancakes make for a delightful and indulgent breakfast, perfect for enjoying with friends and family.

4.7 New Hampshire: Pot Roast

Pot Roast

Introduction to the Dish:

New Hampshire Pot Roast is a comforting and hearty dish that's perfect for a cozy family dinner. It's made by slow-cooking a tender chuck roast with vegetables in a savory broth, resulting in a rich and flavorful meal. This classic recipe is a testament to the delicious and straightforward cuisine found in the heart of New England.

Ingredients:

For the Pot Roast:

- 3-4 pounds chuck roast
- Salt and pepper to taste
- 2 tablespoons vegetable oil
- 1 large onion, chopped
- 2 carrots, sliced
- 2 celery stalks, sliced
- 4 cloves garlic, minced
- 2 cups beef broth
- 1 cup red wine (optional)
- 2 sprigs fresh thyme
- 2 bay leaves
- 4-5 red potatoes, quartered
- 2 cups baby carrots
- Fresh parsley, chopped (for garnish)

For the Gravy (optional):

- 3 tablespoons all-purpose flour
- 3 tablespoons butter

Step-by-Step Instructions:

1. Season and Sear the Roast:

Start by seasoning the chuck roast generously with salt and pepper.

In a large, oven-safe pot or Dutch oven, heat the vegetable oil over medium-high heat. When the oil is hot, add the roast and sear it on all sides until it's nicely browned. This should take about 3-4 minutes per side.

2. Add Aromatics:

Remove the roast and set it aside. In the same pot, add the chopped onion, carrots, celery, and minced garlic. Sauté for about 5 minutes until the vegetables start to soften.

3. Deglaze the Pot:

If using wine, pour it into the pot and scrape up any browned bits from the bottom. Let it simmer for a couple of minutes to cook off the alcohol.

4. Return the Roast:

Place the seared roast back into the pot, nestled among the vegetables.

5. Add Broth and Herbs:

Pour in the beef broth and add the fresh thyme and bay leaves. The roast should be mostly covered with liquid. If not, you can add more broth or water.

6. Braise the Roast:

Cover the pot and transfer it to a preheated oven at 325°F (163°C). Allow the roast to braise in the oven for 2.5 to 3 hours or until it's fork-tender. Check for doneness by testing the meat's tenderness.

7. Add Potatoes and Carrots:

About 45 minutes before the roast is done, add the quartered red potatoes and baby carrots to the pot. Continue cooking until the vegetables are tender.

8. Make the Gravy (Optional):

If you'd like to make gravy, melt butter in a separate saucepan over medium heat, add flour, and whisk until it turns golden brown. Slowly whisk in some of the cooking liquid from the pot roast until the gravy thickens. Season with salt and pepper.

9. Serve:

Remove the bay leaves and thyme sprigs from the pot. Slice the pot roast, serve it with the vegetables, and drizzle with gravy (if desired).
Garnish with freshly chopped parsley.

<u>Tips:</u>

Choose a well-marbled chuck roast for the best results. The marbling will keep the meat tender and add flavor.

The red wine adds depth to the dish, but you can omit it if you prefer not to use alcohol.

You can also customize the vegetables to your liking. Rutabagas, parsnips, and turnips are excellent additions.

Cooking times may vary, so it's essential to check for doneness by testing the meat's tenderness with a fork.

Serve New Hampshire Pot Roast with a side of crusty bread or over mashed potatoes for a classic, comforting meal.

This New Hampshire Pot Roast is a timeless and hearty dish that embodies the flavors of New England cuisine. It's the perfect meal for a family dinner, holiday gathering, or any time you crave a warm and satisfying dish.
Enjoy your "Spinach and Chickpea Power Bowl" as a wholesome and energizing lunch that's both nutritious and delicious!

Steamed Cheeseburgers

Introduction to the Dish:

Connecticut Steamed Cheeseburgers are a unique and delicious regional specialty. These burgers are known for the way the cheese is prepared—steamed to create a creamy and gooey cheese sauce that coats every inch of the burger. If you're a burger enthusiast looking for something different and delightful, you'll want to give this Connecticut classic a try.

Ingredients:

For the Burger:

- 1 pound ground beef (80/20 lean-to-fat ratio recommended)
- Salt and pepper, to taste
- 4 hamburger buns

For the Steamed Cheese Sauce:

- 1/2 cup cheddar cheese, shredded
- 1/2 cup water
- 1 tablespoon cornstarch
- 1 teaspoon dry mustard
- 1/2 teaspoon paprika
- 1/4 teaspoon cayenne pepper (optional for some heat)

For Toppings (Optional):

- Lettuce

Step-by-Step Instructions:

1. Prepare the Burger Patties:

- Divide the ground beef into four equal portions and shape them into burger patties. Season both sides with salt and pepper.

2. Steam the Cheese:

- In a saucepan, combine the shredded cheddar cheese, water, cornstarch, dry mustard, paprika, and cayenne pepper (if using). Stir until the mixture is well combined.
- Heat the saucepan over low heat, stirring constantly, until the cheese mixture becomes smooth and thick. This should take about 5-7 minutes. Once you achieve a creamy cheese sauce, remove it from the heat.

3. Steam the Burger Patties:

- The unique part of steamed cheeseburgers is that the burger patties are also steamed. You can do this by

- Tomato slices
- Onions, sliced
- Pickles

Mustard, ketchup, or your favorite condiments

placing each patty on a rack above a simmering pot of water, or you can use a steamer.

- Steam the burger patties for about 10-15 minutes or until they're cooked to your desired level of doneness.

4. Assemble the Burgers:

- Toast the hamburger buns if you prefer.
- Place the steamed burger patties on the buns.
- Pour the warm steamed cheese sauce over the patties. The sauce should melt over the burger, creating a gooey and cheesy delight.

5. Add Toppings:

- Customize your steamed cheeseburgers with your favorite toppings. Classic choices include lettuce, tomato slices, onions, pickles, and condiments like mustard and ketchup.

6. Serve:

- Serve these unique steamed cheeseburgers hot and enjoy their distinctive and savory flavor

Tips:

Make sure the ground beef is well-seasoned with salt and pepper. The cheese sauce is relatively mild, so seasoning the meat is essential for flavor.

You can use your preferred type of cheese for the sauce. Cheddar is traditional, but feel free to experiment with other cheeses like American, Swiss, or gouda.

Steaming the cheeseburgers gives them a unique texture and flavor. If you don't have a steamer, you can use a DIY setup with a pot of simmering water and a rack or steam basket.

Customize your steamed cheeseburgers with your favorite toppings and condiments. These burgers are highly versatile.

Connecticut Steamed Cheeseburgers are a delightful departure from traditional burgers and offer a unique and satisfying experience. The creamy cheese sauce and perfectly steamed patties make them a must-try for burger aficionados and food explorers alike.

4.9 Delaware: Chicken and Slippery Dumplings

Chicken and Slippery Dumplings

Introduction to the Dish:

Delaware Chicken and Slippery Dumplings is a comforting and hearty dish with tender chunks of chicken and soft, dumplings that are "slippery" due to their smooth texture. It's a classic recipe that's perfect for warming up on a chilly day and is often enjoyed as a soul-soothing meal.

Ingredients:

For the Chicken:

- 1 whole chicken (about 3-4 pounds), cut into pieces
- Salt and pepper, to taste
- 2 tablespoons vegetable oil
- 1 onion, chopped
- 2 carrots, chopped
- 2 celery stalks, chopped
- 2 cloves garlic, minced
- 8 cups chicken broth
- 2 bay leaves
- 1 teaspoon dried thyme
- 1/4 cup fresh parsley, chopped
- 2 cups all-purpose flour

For the Dumplings:

Step-by-Step Instructions:

1. Cook the Chicken:

Season the chicken pieces with salt and pepper.

In a large pot or Dutch oven, heat the vegetable oil over medium-high heat. Add the chicken pieces and brown them on all sides. Remove the chicken and set it aside.

2. Sauté the Vegetables:

In the same pot, add the chopped onion, carrots, and celery. Sauté for about 5 minutes until the vegetables are softened. Add the minced garlic and cook for another minute.

3. Add Broth and Seasoning:

Return the browned chicken to the pot. Pour in the chicken broth and add the bay leaves, dried thyme, and half of the chopped parsley.

- 2 cups all-purpose flour
- 1 teaspoon baking powder
- 1/2 teaspoon salt
- 1/4 cup unsalted butter, cold and cubed
- 3/4 cup milk

Bring the mixture to a boil, then reduce the heat to a simmer. Cover and cook for about 30-40 minutes or until the chicken is tender.

4. Make the Dumplings:

While the chicken is cooking, prepare the dumplings. In a mixing bowl, combine the flour, baking powder, and salt. Add the cold, cubed butter, and use a pastry cutter or fork to cut it into the dry ingredients until it resembles coarse crumbs.

Pour in the milk and stir until just combined. Be careful not to overmix; the dough should be sticky.

5. Add Dumplings:

After the chicken is tender, drop spoonfuls of the dumpling dough into the simmering broth. Cover the pot and let the dumplings cook for about 15-20 minutes until they are cooked through. They will become soft and "slippery."

6. Serve:

Once the dumplings are cooked, remove the bay leaves and discard them.

Serve the Chicken and Slippery Dumplings hot, garnished with the remaining chopped parsley.

<u>**Tips:**</u>

You can customize the dumplings by adding fresh herbs, such as chopped parsley or thyme, to the dough for extra flavor.

If the dough is too sticky to handle, lightly flour your hands when shaping the dumplings.

Some variations of this dish include adding vegetables like peas or corn for extra color and flavor.

Delaware Chicken and Slippery Dumplings is a warm and filling meal that's perfect for family dinners or when you want a comforting dish to lift your spirits. The tender chicken and soft dumplings are sure to make it a favorite in your home.

4.10 Maryland: Maryland Crab Cakes

Maryland Crab Cakes

Introduction to the Dish:

Maryland Crab Cakes are a beloved regional specialty known for their delicious taste and simplicity. These crab cakes feature lump crabmeat mixed with flavorful seasonings and binding ingredients. They're typically pan-fried until golden brown, creating a delectable crispy exterior and a tender, sweet, and flaky interior.

Ingredients:

- 1 pound lump crabmeat, picked over for shells
- 1/3 cup mayonnaise
- 1 large egg
- 1 1/2 teaspoons Dijon mustard
- 1 1/2 teaspoons Old Bay seasoning (or your favorite seafood seasoning)
- 1 teaspoon Worcestershire sauce
- 1 teaspoon lemon juice
- 1/2 teaspoon salt
- 1/4 teaspoon black pepper
- 1/4 cup finely chopped fresh parsley
- 1/2 cup breadcrumbs
- Vegetable oil, for frying

Step-by-Step Instructions:

1. Prepare the Crab Cakes:

In a large mixing bowl, combine the mayonnaise, egg, Dijon mustard, Old Bay seasoning, Worcestershire sauce, lemon juice, salt, and pepper. Mix these ingredients until they are well combined.

2. Add Crabmeat:

Gently fold in the lump crabmeat. Be careful not to break up the crabmeat too much. You want to maintain those delicious lumps.

3. Add Parsley and Breadcrumbs:

Mix in the finely chopped parsley and breadcrumbs. The breadcrumbs help bind the mixture and add a bit of texture.

4. Form the Crab Cakes:

With clean hands, divide the crab mixture into equal portions. Shape them into crab cakes, about 3 inches in diameter. You can make them as thick or thin as you prefer.

5. Chill the Crab Cakes:

Place the crab cakes on a baking sheet or platter and refrigerate them for at least 1 hour. Chilling helps the crab cakes hold their shape.

6. Fry the Crab Cakes:

In a large skillet, heat vegetable oil over medium-high heat. When the oil is hot (around 350°F or until a small piece of bread sizzles when dropped in), carefully add the crab cakes. Fry them for about 3-4 minutes on each side or until they are golden brown and crispy.

7. Drain and Serve:

Use a slotted spatula to remove the crab cakes from the skillet and place them on paper towels to drain any excess oil.

8. Serve:

Maryland Crab Cakes are best served hot and fresh. You can enjoy them as a main course with a side of coleslaw, remoulade sauce, or tartar sauce. They are also great in sandwiches or as an appetizer.

Tips:

Use fresh lump crabmeat whenever possible for the best flavor and texture.

The Old Bay seasoning is a key flavor element in Maryland Crab Cakes. If you can't find Old Bay, use your favorite seafood seasoning, but Old Bay is recommended for an authentic taste.

Don't overcrowd the pan when frying the crab cakes. Fry them in batches if necessary.

Maryland Crab Cakes are a Chesapeake Bay tradition, and they capture the essence of Maryland's love for seafood. Enjoy these delectable crab cakes as a taste of the Mid-Atlantic region's culinary heritage.

4.11 Michigan: Pasties

Pasties

Introduction to the Dish:

Michigan Pasties are a beloved Upper Midwest tradition, particularly in the Upper Peninsula of Michigan. They are hearty, hand-held pies filled with a delicious combination of meats and vegetables. Pasties were initially brought to the region by Cornish miners and have become a staple comfort food.

Ingredients:

For the Pastry:

- 3 cups all-purpose flour
- 1 1/2 teaspoons salt
- 1 cup unsalted butter, cold and cubed
- 1/2 cup ice-cold water

For the Filling:

- 1 pound ground beef
- 1/2 pound ground pork
- 1 large onion, finely chopped
- 2 large potatoes, peeled and diced
- 1 turnip, peeled and diced
- 1 carrot, peeled and diced
- Salt and pepper to taste
- Butter, for brushing

Step-by-Step Instructions:

1. Prepare the Pastry:

For the Pastry:

- In a large bowl, combine the flour and salt.
- Add the cold, cubed butter and use a pastry cutter or your fingers to work the butter into the flour until the mixture resembles coarse crumbs.
- Gradually add the ice-cold water and mix until the dough comes together.
- Divide the dough into 6 equal portions, form them into discs, wrap in plastic wrap, and refrigerate for about 30 minutes.

2. Make the Filling:

- In a large mixing bowl, combine the ground beef, ground pork, chopped onions, diced potatoes, diced turnip, and diced carrot.
- Season the filling mixture with salt and pepper to taste.

3. Assemble the Pasties:

- Preheat your oven to 350°F (175°C).
- Roll out each pastry disc into a circle, about 1/8 inch thick.
- Place a portion of the filling on one half of each pastry circle.

- Fold the other half of the pastry over the filling to create a half-moon shape.
- Crimp the edges to seal the pasties.
- Cut a small slit in the top of each pasty to allow steam to escape.
- Brush each pasty with a bit of butter.

4. Bake the Pasties:

- Place the pasties on a baking sheet lined with parchment paper.
- Bake in the preheated oven for about 45-60 minutes, or until they are golden brown.

5. Serve:

- Let the pasties cool slightly before serving. They can be enjoyed warm or at room temperature.

<u>Tips:</u>

Pasties can be made in advance and frozen. Just wrap them well and store them in the freezer. When you're ready to enjoy them, bake from frozen, adding a little extra time to the baking.

You can customize the filling with other vegetables or herbs of your choice, but the traditional combination remains a favorite.

Michigan Pasties are a delightful and hearty meal that's perfect for lunch or dinner. Enjoy this Upper Midwest comfort food straight from your own kitchen!

4.12 Indiana: Hoosier Fried Pork Sandwich

Hoosier Fried Pork Sandwich

Introduction to the Dish:

The Hoosier Fried Pork Sandwich is an iconic dish in Indiana. This delicious sandwich features a breaded and fried pork tenderloin, usually larger than the bun, and is typically served with fresh vegetables and condiments. It's a beloved comfort food in the Hoosier state.

Ingredients:

For the Pork Tenderloin:

- 4 boneless pork loin chops
- Salt and pepper, to taste
- 1 cup all-purpose flour
- 2 large eggs
- 2 cups breadcrumbs (preferably Panko)
- Vegetable oil for frying

For the Sandwich:

- 4 hamburger buns or sandwich rolls
- Lettuce leaves
- Sliced tomatoes
- Sliced onions
- Pickles
- Mustard and mayonnaise (optional)
- Ketchup (optional)

Step-by-Step Instructions:

1. Prepare the Pork Tenderloin:

- Start by pounding the pork chops to an even thickness (about 1/4 to 1/2 inch) using a meat mallet or rolling pin. This helps the pork cook evenly.
- Season the pork chops with salt and pepper on both sides.

2. Set Up a Breading Station:

- In separate shallow dishes, place the flour, beaten eggs, and breadcrumbs.
- Dredge each pork chop in the flour, shaking off the excess.
- Dip the floured pork chop in the beaten eggs, ensuring it's coated.
- Finally, press the pork chop into the breadcrumbs, making sure it's well coated. Press the breadcrumbs onto the pork gently.

3. Fry the Pork Tenderloin:

- In a large skillet or deep fryer, heat about 1 inch of vegetable oil to 350°F (175°C).

- Carefully add the breaded pork chops to the hot oil (you may need to do this in batches) and fry until they are golden brown and cooked through, which should take about 3-4 minutes per side.
- Once done, transfer the fried pork chops to a paper towel-lined plate to drain excess oil.

4. Assemble the Sandwich:

- To assemble the Hoosier Fried Pork Sandwich, start with the bottom half of the hamburger bun.
- Place a lettuce leaf on the bun, followed by a fried pork tenderloin.
- Top the pork with slices of tomato, onion, and pickles.
- If desired, you can add mustard, mayonnaise, and ketchup to the bun.
- Finish by adding the top half of the bun.

5. Serve:

- Serve the Hoosier Fried Pork Sandwich immediately while it's still warm and crispy.

Tips:

You can customize your sandwich with your favorite condiments and toppings. Coleslaw is another common addition in some variations.

If you prefer a spicier version, you can add hot sauce or hot pepper rings.

Pair this sandwich with classic Hoosier sides like onion rings or french fries.

Enjoy your Indiana Hoosier Fried Pork Sandwich, a delectable and filling meal that's a staple in the state!

4.13 Illinois: Chicago-Style Hot Dog

Chicago-Style Hot Dog

Introduction to the Dish:

The Chicago-Style Hot Dog is an iconic street food in Illinois, particularly in Chicago. It's a delicious and colorful ensemble of flavors and textures that make it unique. This hot dog is all about the toppings, and each ingredient plays a vital role in creating this mouthwatering masterpiece.

Ingredients:

For the Hot Dog:

- 4 beef hot dog sausages
- 4 poppy seed hot dog buns
- Yellow mustard
- Neon green sweet pickle relish
- Chopped onions
- Tomato slices
- Pickle spears
- Sport peppers
- Celery salt

Step-by-Step Instructions:

1. Steam or Grill the Hot Dogs:

- You can either steam or grill the beef hot dog sausages. Steaming is the traditional method, but grilling imparts a delicious smoky flavor.
- Cook the hot dogs until they're heated through and have a nice, slightly crispy texture.

2. Prepare the Toppings:

- While the hot dogs are cooking, prepare the toppings.
- Dice the onions and slice the tomatoes.
- Pickle spears and sport peppers are typically used whole.

3. Assemble the Chicago-Style Hot Dog:

- Take a poppy seed hot dog bun and add a drizzle of yellow mustard along the inside.
- Place the cooked hot dog sausage in the bun.
- Add a generous portion of neon green sweet pickle relish, giving the dog a vibrant green appearance.
- Sprinkle diced onions over the relish.

- Place two slices of tomato on top.
- Add a pickle spear and a sport pepper.
- Finish with a sprinkle of celery salt for an extra layer of flavor.

4. Serve:

- Your Chicago-Style Hot Dog is now ready to be served.
- The key to enjoying it fully is not to overdress it. The balance of flavors and textures is what makes it so special.

Tips:

Use high-quality beef hot dog sausages for an authentic Chicago taste.

If you can't find neon green sweet pickle relish, you can mix regular sweet pickle relish with a drop or two of green food coloring.

Sport peppers are small, spicy pickled peppers. If you can't find them, you can use sliced jalapeños for a similar kick.

The Chicago-Style Hot Dog is traditionally served with a side of crinkle-cut french fries.

Enjoy your Chicago-Style Hot Dog, an Illinois classic that's famous for its combination of flavors and toppings!

4.14 Wisconsin: Beer Brats

Beer Brats

Introduction to the Dish:

Wisconsin Beer Brats are a beloved Midwest classic. These flavorful bratwurst sausages are simmered in beer with onions and spices, then grilled to perfection. They are traditionally served with a variety of toppings and a side of sauerkraut.

Ingredients:

For the Beer Brats:

- 6 fresh bratwurst sausages
- 2 large onions, sliced
- 2 bottles (24 ounces) of your favorite beer (lager or pilsner)
- 2 tablespoons vegetable oil
- 2 cloves garlic, minced
- 1 teaspoon caraway seeds
- 6 bratwurst buns

For Toppings:

- Mustard
- Sauerkraut
- Ketchup
- Sliced pickles

Step-by-Step Instructions:

1. Sear the Brats:

Heat the vegetable oil in a large skillet or on the grates of your grill.

Sear the brats on all sides until they are browned, about 5 minutes. This step is to lock in the juices.

2. Simmer the Brats:

In a large pot or aluminum tray, add the sliced onions, minced garlic, and caraway seeds.

Place the seared brats on top of the onions.

Pour in the beer, making sure the brats are fully submerged.

Bring the beer to a gentle simmer, then reduce the heat and let the brats cook for about 20-30 minutes. This will infuse them with beer flavor and make them tender.

3. Grill the Brats:

Preheat your grill to medium-high heat.

Remove the brats from the beer mixture and grill them for about 5-10 minutes, turning occasionally until they are nicely browned and have grill marks.

4. Serve:

Place each beer brat in a bratwurst bun.

Add your choice of toppings. Common choices include mustard, sauerkraut, ketchup, and sliced pickles.

Serve the Wisconsin Beer Brats while hot and enjoy!

Tips:

Use a good-quality beer to impart flavor to the brats. A lager or pilsner works well.

You can toast the bratwurst buns on the grill for a minute or two for added flavor.

Be creative with your toppings. Wisconsin locals often enjoy their beer brats with unique combinations like cream cheese, jalapeños, and more.

Enjoy your Wisconsin Beer Brats, a delicious and hearty dish perfect for grilling season and tailgating parties!

Tater Tot Hotdish

Introduction to the Dish:

Tater Tot Hotdish, often referred to as Minnesota's unofficial state casserole, is the epitome of comfort food. This classic Midwestern dish is a hearty and delicious combination of ground beef, creamy soups, mixed vegetables, and crispy tater tots.

Ingredients:

- Assorted fresh vegetables (carrots, celery, cucumbers, bell peppers, cherry tomatoes, etc.)
- 1 cup of your favorite hummus
- Fresh herbs (parsley, cilantro, or dill) for garnish (optional)
- Olive oil for drizzling (optional)
- Lemon juice for drizzling (optional)
- Salt and pepper to taste (optional)

Step-by-Step Instructions:

1. Preheat the Oven:

Preheat your oven to 375°F (190°C).

2. Brown the Ground Beef:

In a large skillet, cook the ground beef and chopped onion over medium-high heat until the meat is browned and the onions are translucent. Drain any excess grease.

3. Season the Meat:

Stir in the minced garlic and season with salt and pepper to taste.

4. Add Soups and Vegetables:

In a large mixing bowl, combine the browned beef and onions, cream of mushroom soup, cream of celery soup, and the frozen mixed vegetables. Mix until well combined.

5. Layer in a Casserole Dish:

Transfer the mixture into a 9x13-inch baking dish or casserole dish, spreading it evenly.

6. Layer with Tater Tots:

Arrange the frozen tater tots in a single layer over the meat and vegetable mixture.

7. Bake:

Place the casserole dish in the preheated oven and bake for 35-45 minutes, or until the tater tots are golden brown, and the hotdish is bubbling.

8. Add Cheese and Bake Again:

Remove the dish from the oven and sprinkle the shredded cheddar cheese evenly over the tater tots.
Return the casserole to the oven and bake for an additional 5-10 minutes, or until the cheese is melted and bubbly.

9. Serve:

Allow it to cool for a few minutes before serving. Enjoy your comforting Minnesota Tater Tot Hotdish!

Tips:

You can add other ingredients such as diced green beans, mushrooms, or Worcestershire sauce for additional flavor.

Feel free to customize your Tater Tot Hotdish with your favorite seasonings or spices.

This dish is perfect for potlucks, family gatherings, and cold winter nights.

Minnesota's Tater Tot Hotdish is a beloved classic, and it's sure to warm your heart and satisfy your taste buds. Enjoy!

4.16 Iowa: Loose Meat Sandwich

Loose Meat Sandwich

Introduction to the Dish:

"Banana and Oatmeal Cookies" are a delightful and guilt-free sweet treat that's perfect for satisfying your cookie cravings. These cookies are naturally sweetened with ripe bananas and honey, and they're packed with wholesome oats. Whether you enjoy them as a snack or dessert, these cookies are quick to make and a healthier alternative to traditional cookies.

Ingredients:

- 1 pound ground beef
- 1 small onion, finely chopped
- 1/4 cup water
- 1 tablespoon yellow mustard
- 1 tablespoon brown sugar
- 1 tablespoon Worcestershire sauce
- Salt and pepper to taste
- Hamburger buns for serving

Step-by-Step Instructions:

1. Brown the Ground Beef:

In a large skillet over medium-high heat, add the ground beef and chopped onion.
Cook the beef and onions, breaking up the meat into crumbles as it cooks until it's browned and the onions are translucent.

2. Season the Meat:

Add the water, yellow mustard, brown sugar, Worcestershire sauce, salt, and pepper to the cooked beef. Stir to combine.

3. Simmer:

Reduce the heat to low and let the mixture simmer for about 10-15 minutes, allowing the flavors to meld and the liquid to reduce.

4. Assemble the Sandwiches:

Split the hamburger buns and lightly toast them if desired.
Spoon the loose meat mixture onto the bottom half of each bun.

5. Serve:

Serve the Iowa Loose Meat Sandwiches with your favorite toppings, such as pickles, onions, ketchup, and mustard.

Tips:

Customize your sandwich with various toppings like cheese, lettuce, or diced tomatoes.

Maid-Rites are known for their loose meat filling, so don't worry if it's not as saucy as a traditional sloppy joe.

If you prefer, you can use lean ground beef to reduce the fat content.

Iowa's Loose Meat Sandwich is a savory, satisfying classic that captures the essence of the American Midwest. Enjoy this unique and delicious sandwich!

4.17 Missouri: St. Louis Toasted Ravioli

St. Louis Toasted Ravioli:

Introduction to the Dish:

St. Louis Toasted Ravioli is a beloved appetizer or snack that originated in St. Louis, Missouri. This dish features crispy, breaded ravioli served with a flavorful marinara sauce. It's perfect for sharing with friends and family or as a unique treat for yourself.

Ingredients:

For the Toasted Ravioli:

- 1 package (about 24) frozen or fresh cheese ravioli
- 2 cups breadcrumbs
- 1/2 cup grated Parmesan cheese
- 2 large eggs
- 1/4 cup milk
- 1 teaspoon dried Italian seasoning
- 1/2 teaspoon garlic powder
- Salt and pepper to taste
- Vegetable oil for frying

For the Marinara Sauce:

- 1 28-ounce can crushed tomatoes
- 2 cloves garlic, minced

Step-by-Step Instructions:

1. Prepare the Marinara Sauce:

- In a saucepan, combine the crushed tomatoes, minced garlic, basil, oregano, salt, and pepper.
- Simmer over low heat, stirring occasionally, while you prepare the toasted ravioli.

2. Bread the Ravioli:

- In a shallow dish, combine breadcrumbs, grated Parmesan cheese, dried Italian seasoning, garlic powder, salt, and pepper.
- In another shallow dish, whisk together the eggs and milk.
- Take each ravioli, dip it into the egg mixture, allowing any excess to drip off, and then coat it with the breadcrumb mixture. Place the breaded ravioli on a baking sheet.

3. Heat the Oil:

- In a large, deep skillet, heat about 2 inches of vegetable oil over medium-high heat. You can also use a deep fryer if you have one. Heat the oil to 350°F (175°C).

4. Fry the Ravioli:

- 1 teaspoon dried basil
- 1 teaspoon dried oregano
- Salt and pepper to taste

- Carefully add the breaded ravioli to the hot oil in batches, making sure not to overcrowd the pan.
- Fry for about 2-3 minutes per side, or until they are golden brown and crispy. Remove them using a slotted spoon and place them on paper towels to drain excess oil.

5. Serve:

- Serve the St. Louis Toasted Ravioli with the marinara sauce on the side for dipping.

Tips:

Be cautious when frying the ravioli to avoid oil splatters.

You can adjust the seasoning to your taste in both the marinara sauce and the breadcrumb mixture.

To make the dish even more authentic, sprinkle the finished ravioli with additional grated Parmesan cheese before serving.

St. Louis Toasted Ravioli is a delightful, crunchy, and flavorful appetizer that's sure to be a hit at any gathering or as a tasty snack. Enjoy the taste of St. Louis at home!

4.18 North Dakota: Knoephla Soup

Knoephla Soup

Introduction to the Dish:

Knoephla Soup is a comforting and hearty soup that hails from North Dakota. It features soft and chewy dumplings made from a simple dough, which are added to a creamy chicken or vegetable broth with vegetables. This soup is perfect for warming up during cold North Dakota winters.

Ingredients:

For the Knoephla Dough:

- 2 cups all-purpose flour
- 1/2 cup milk
- 1 egg
- 1/2 teaspoon salt

For the Soup:

- 6 cups chicken or vegetable broth
- 2 cups potatoes, peeled and diced
- 1 cup carrots, diced
- 1/2 cup celery, diced
- 1/2 cup onion, finely chopped
- 1/2 cup butter
- 2 cups half-and-half or whole milk
- 2 cups cooked chicken, shredded (optional)
  - Salt and pepper to taste

Step-by-Step Instructions:

1. Make the Knoephla Dough:

- In a mixing bowl, combine the flour and salt.
- In a separate bowl, beat the egg and milk.
- Gradually add the wet ingredients to the dry ingredients, mixing until a stiff dough forms.
- Knead the dough on a floured surface until it's smooth. Roll it out to about 1/8 inch thickness.
- Cut the dough into small squares or diamond shapes (approximately 1/2 inch).

2. Prepare the Soup:

- In a large pot, melt the butter over medium heat.
- Add the chopped onion, carrots, and celery. Sauté until they are tender, about 5 minutes.
- Pour in the chicken or vegetable broth and add the diced potatoes. Bring the mixture to a boil and then reduce the heat to a simmer. Cook until the potatoes are soft, about 15-20 minutes.
- If you're using cooked chicken, add it to the soup now.
- Pour in the half-and-half (or whole milk) and stir well.

- Chopped fresh parsley for garnish (optional)
- Drop the knoephla dough pieces into the soup. Simmer for an additional 10-15 minutes, or until the dumplings are tender and have floated to the surface.
- Season the soup with salt and pepper to taste.

3. Serve:

- Ladle the warm and comforting Knoephla Soup into bowls.
- Garnish with chopped fresh parsley if desired.
- Serve hot and enjoy!

Tips:

If you find the dough is too sticky to work with, you can lightly flour your hands and work surface to prevent sticking.

Knoephla Soup is often made with chicken, but you can make a vegetarian version by using vegetable broth and omitting the chicken.

Adjust the thickness of the soup by adding more or less half-and-half or milk to your preference.

Knoephla Soup is a delightful and filling dish that embodies the warmth and comfort of North Dakota. It's a great choice for a hearty meal, especially during the cold winter months. Enjoy this taste of North Dakota!

CONCLUSION

In conclusion, I would like to express my sincere gratitude to all the readers who have purchased and explored "The Ultimate American Cookbook: A Treasury of Recipes." We hope that this culinary journey through the diverse and delicious flavors of American cuisine has been a rewarding and delightful experience for you.

Cooking is not just about preparing food; it's about creating memories, sharing moments with loved ones, and savoring the cultural richness that each dish brings to the table. The recipes in this book are a celebration of American culinary traditions, from coast to coast. Whether you've tried one recipe or many, we hope you've found joy in the art of cooking and have created memorable meals for your family and friends.

Your support and interest in this cookbook are greatly appreciated. We hope it continues to be a source of inspiration in your kitchen, and that you enjoy many more delicious adventures in the world of American cuisine.

Thank you once again for choosing "The Ultimate American Cookbook." Happy cooking!